nobu THE cookbook

nobu THE cookbook

Nobuyuki Matsuhisa

Photographs by **Fumihiko Watanabe**

Translation by Laura Holland

KODANSHA INTERNATIONAL
Tokyo • New York • London

WASALABY—a Tokyo store that specializes in contemporary Japanese ceramics with a mild Western influence—was kind enough to lend us some stunning pieces by the potters Taizo Kuroda and Yutaka Hanaoka for use in this book.

Taizo Kuroda's white dishes were used for Abalone with Wasabi Pepper Sauce (page 26), Sea Urchin Tempura (page 40), Spinach-Wrapped Sea Urchin with Egg Sauce (page 43), Scampi with Spicy Lemon Garlic Sauce (page 51), Spicy Octopus Salad (page 70), Grilled Octopus with Miso Anticucho Sauce (page 78), Squid Pasta with Light Garlic Sauce (page 82), Baked Monkfish Medley with Tosa-zu (page 103), Seafood Ceviche, Nobu Style (page 119), Black Cod with Miso (page 125) and Tomato Ceviche, Nobu Style (page 152).

Yutaka Hanaoka's black dishes were used for Abalone Shabu-shabu with Egg Sauce and Caviar (page 30), Scallops with Creamy Spicy Sauce (page 36), Kuruma Shrimp Tempura with Creamy Spicy Sauce (page 53), Frothing Blue Crab (page 65), Octopus Shabu-shabu with Spicy Ume Sauce (page 77), Baby Squid Tempura with Squid Ink Sauce (page 85), Asparagus and Salmon Roe with Egg Sauce (page 151) and Sea Eel Dragon Roll and Sushi (page 165).

Distributed in the United States by Kodansha America, Inc. 575 Lexington Avenue, New York, New York 10022.

Published by Kodansha International Ltd., 17–14 Otowa 1-chome, Bunkyo-ku, Tokyo 112–8652 and Kodansha America, Inc.
Text copyright © 2001 by Nobuyuki Matsuhisa.
Photographs copyright © 2001 by Fumihiko Watanabe.
Translation copyright © 2001 by Kodansha International Ltd.
All rights reserved. Printed in Japan.

ISBN 4-7700-2533-5

First Edition, 2001
03 04 05   10 9 8 7 6 5 4

www.thejapanpage.com

C O N T E N T S

Dear Nobu,

It seems like only a short time ago we met
and shared a saké at Matsuhisa, your first
restaurant. You prepared a dinner for us that
was so special that I hoped one day we could
do something together. Now we are partners
in several Nobu restaurants and people
all over the world can enjoy your food.

I'm so proud of your success and I want to
congratulate you on a fine cookbook. The photos
of your food are terrific. But most important,
I think, is the story of how you started and who
inspired you along the way. It gives insight
into who Nobu Matsuhisa is, as well as the
journey you took to get where you are today.
You are one of the world's great chefs.

I want to wish you great success with this book
and all future endeavors.

Your friend and partner,

FOREWORD

THERE ARE MANY ADJECTIVES one can use to describe a fine chef: passionate, curious, facile, knowledgeable, adventuresome, inventive, well-trained and daring. Add to this list the adjective "entrepreneurial" and "fine chef" can become "great chef." There are not very many "great chefs" in the world—only a few exist anywhere at any one time, but Nobu Matsuhisa certainly belongs in that category. With ease and grace and invisible, intelligent cunning, he turns the simplest ingredients into masterpieces of complexity. When one eats "Nobu food" one knows that years of training and years of thinking and years of tradition have contributed to the particular creation one is savoring.

Personally, I consider Japanese cuisine one of my favorites. I started to eat "*tatami*-style" many years ago when I went to college in New York City. There were just a handful of Japanese restaurants in the city, and each was unique and delicious: One styled its menu after the food of Kyoto, another made only tempura, another only sushi and sashimi. I frequented these restaurants several times a week, trying every single dish on every single menu. As more and more Japanese families opened small and beautifully crafted eateries in the city, I ferreted them out and compared preparation styles and was soon able to distinguish the real, the careful, the best, from all other dishes. Several trips to Japan—to Tokyo, Yakushima, Naoshima, Nagano, the Izu Peninsula and Osaka—enabled me to become more educated and discriminating.

On a trip to Los Angeles I was treated to the most superb Japanese food I had ever tasted in the United States. Prepared in front of me by a quiet and handsome man called simply Nobu, I was entranced and elated that the foods I had sampled in Japan were now available in America.

Nobu never disappoints. His restaurants are well run, impeccably designed and lovely to dine in. His menus are extraordinary and enticing. His personal demeanor is friendly and charming. He has changed the karma of Japanese food for me forever. Now I look not just at the sushi—I examine every grain of rice and test the crunchiness and freshness of the *nori*, examine the variety and cut of the fish, taste the *o-shinko* and the *wasabi*, and marvel at the unique and flavorful combinations. Nobu changed cod for me forever, and his spiny lobster soup is second to none. In fact I had not tasted a broth as wonderful or a lobster as tender on any foray in Japan!

I am so pleased and so excited that now Nobu has collected a great number of his creations, techniques and classic recipes in one very beautiful volume. And I will always remember what Nobu told me about his cooking: It may look simple and take just minutes to prepare, but one has to consider how long it took to make the *konbu*, pickle the eggplant, dry the bonito and press the *nori*—ingredients that are essential to so many traditional Japanese recipes.

Martha Stewart

INTRODUCTION

COOKING IS MY LIFE and this book is a straightforward and honest expression of that life—of me as a man and a chef. I give you my way of cooking freely and show you exactly how each dish is prepared and served in my restaurants. Some friends have questioned the wisdom of making these recipes accessible to the general public. They think, perhaps, that my business could be damaged in some way by revealing professional secrets. But cooking isn't like that. Food is imbued with the feelings and personality of the cook. Even if you were to follow my instructions faithfully, using precise amounts of identical ingredients, I am quite sure that you would never be able to perfectly recreate the same flavors and textures that I make. For I always put something special in my food—my heart, or *kokoro* as we say in Japanese—and, you, of course, must put your own heart into your own cooking.

When I stand in the kitchen, I'm driven by one basic desire: to delight and satisfy my customers and to hear them say they have enjoyed an excellent meal. I know there are many chefs who are either technically or artistically better than me. But I also know that my food has soul. For me, cooking is most about giving my customers little surprises that will lead them to make discoveries about their own latent tastes. It's about communicating my *kokoro* through every single dish I make. If this book inspires you to try out some of the recipes and gain new insights into your own way of cooking, I will be more than happy. Because that too would be another way of communicating my *kokoro* through cooking.

People often ask me to define my food. I call it "Nobu-style" cuisine. It's firmly based on Japanese cooking—fundamentally sushi—but with North and South American influences. My intention has always been to draw on the very best of Japanese cooking in my own individual style. Such has been the aim of this book, too, and for this reason I have made no compromises with the ingredients used to create the recipes—nothing but fresh, quality seafood and many ingredients that can only be found in Japan. Nobu-style cuisine is all about bringing out the best in the freshest seafood and drawing out the natural sweetness and textures of vegetables. Fish should always be fresh enough to eat raw. Shellfish, crustaceans and octopus should always, ideally, be bought when still alive. No seasoning—however subtle—can quite match real freshness. Taste the difference for yourself!

It goes without saying that the basics will only provide you with a foundation on which to build your cooking skills. The rest is really up to you. And what could be more fun than discovering your own distinct flavors? Nobu-style cuisine is based on sushi: I know how to cook rice well, how to choose the best fish and how to prepare and serve it. But it doesn't stop there. The important thing—and not just in cooking—is to adapt and apply the basics and to keep on experimenting with new ideas. In this way, Nobu-style cuisine is continually evolving. Don't worry if you don't get it right the first time. Try it over and over again and see for yourself whether you like your *toro* well-done or rare, and look for the exact degree of saltiness or spiciness to suit your palate. In time, any one of the recipes in this book could evolve into your own inimitable dish.

And don't forget to add plenty of *kokoro*!

ACKNOWLEDGMENTS

When I cook, I always imagine I'm in front of a stretch of blank canvas. The dishes I paint, so to speak, must be a vibrant and energetic balance of color and flavor. A chef's work is ephemeral: for all the passion and attention he puts into making a dish, it disappears at the touch of a pair of chopsticks. My likening cooking to painting may sound pompous, but the intensity that's required of the chef in each moment of the cooking process has never ceased to mesmerize me. When I turned fifty, I felt that it was time to write a book that would serve as a lasting record of my work.

All the photographs of food were taken in Tokyo. I wanted to make the book in Tokyo because I was born and raised in Japan, and in 1998, when I started on this project, I happened to be there once every month for the opening of a new restaurant, Nobu Tokyo. Moreover, I knew from working with seafood and vegetables from all over the world that Tokyo offered first-class ingredients in terms of quality and selection.

On the days of the shoots, the work of J.J. and Ishii in securing the ingredients I needed was vital. They never complained, even when I made sudden requests on the actual morning of a shoot, and somehow always managed to provide me with top-notch seafood from Tsukiji market. It is because of them, along with the close cooperation of my Nobu Tokyo staff, that I was able to do what I set out to do: make the very best dishes using the very best ingredients. Here I would like to thank them, as I would Eriko Hirai for writing the "Nobu Matsuhisa Story" (overleaf), and Tomoko Sekikawa for listening to my rambling thoughts on cooking and food in general and making enough sense of them to write all the recipes in this book.

The wonderful staff at my publisher and its parent company, Paul Hulbert and Shimon Yamaguchi, who took care of everything from arranging the photo shoots to editing the text, and Laura Holland, the translator, all made this project a rewarding experience for me. I was also fortunate in having as a designer Kazuhiko Miki, who made the text and the photos come to life on paper, and the photographer Fumihiko Watanabe, who captured my work on film with consummate skill. With them, and with the help of Hokusetsu, the saké brewery, I was able to have photos taken of my other restaurants throughout the world (although unfortunately Ubon by Nobu in London, and the restaurants in Milan and Miami, were not yet open when I toured Europe and the United States with Miki and Watanabe).

This book took two years to complete, and it was no easy task. Every page bears witness to the teamwork that went into creating it. Though *Nobu* is just one book among many, for me it is a source of renewed energy. It represents the same values that I maintain at my restaurants: good food, good service and teamwork.

By visiting Tokyo every month, I was able to catch up with my mother, eighty-nine years old and still in good health. She had a profound influence on my career as a chef, and for that I dedicate this book to her. I also dedicate it to my father, who left me a photograph that first inspired me to venture overseas.

Others, too, have supported or inspired me: my two daughters, in Tokyo and in London, and my wife Yoko, who kept Matsuhisa in Los Angeles running while I was away; Mr. and Mrs. Nakane of Matsuei Sushi, who first taught me how to make sushi; my rock-star friend Eikichi Yazawa, who introduced me to Hokusetsu's saké; and Robert De Niro, Kenny G, Martha Stewart and Ken Takakura, all of whom graciously helped me despite their busy schedules.

Finally, to my staff throughout the world, to all the chefs who are an inspiration to me, and to my friends—this book, my life even, wouldn't have been possible without you. I take this opportunity to thank all of you from the bottom of my heart.

THE NOBU MATSUHISA STORY

An unforgettable night

There is one night that for me is unforgettable, one scene that I can't get out of my mind. It is branded onto my eyes. To remember what happened that night is to remember despair. Even now, the memory is as vivid as the events of yesterday. It was the hardest night I ever lived through. But perhaps because of it, I learned to be thankful and to find the courage to take a sure step forward.

Anchorage, in a whirl of light snow. In that increasingly snowbound town, silver with the settling flakes, flames shot up in an orange blaze. I stood rooted under the falling snow, silently watching the building burn down. Having rushed to the scene from a party at a friend's house, I was only wearing a T-shirt, yet I didn't feel the cold, nor anything else. The cinders from the burning building flew up into the sky, and some landed on my cheeks. They must have been hot, but I wasn't conscious of it at the time.

It was my restaurant that was burning; it had only been fifty days since it opened. In the six months before opening day, I had personally gone into the building with a hammer and saw to help with the construction. I had secured supply channels for ingredients, thought up a menu, and had even been coaching the staff. When the restaurant opened, it was very well received; day in and day out, it was always full.

I had worked for fifty days without taking any time off. I had accumulated debts in order to open the restaurant, but I felt encouraged by the way things were going. I figured I was making enough money for my wife and daughter, whom I'd left behind in Japan, to come and live with me. So I sent for them.

That fiftieth day was Thanksgiving. I had closed the restaurant with the intention of giving the staff and myself a break. We had all worked nonstop until then.

It was while I was having a good time at a party that night that I received a telephone call from my partner in the restaurant. "Nobu, the restaurant's on fire! Come as quickly as you can," he said in a panicky voice. I thought it was a sick joke and told him so, but he repeated, "There's a fire. Really, there is." As we talked on the phone, I began to hear sirens. Apparently it was true.

I borrowed my friend's car and rushed over. Even if there was a fire, it couldn't be a serious one; by the time I arrived, they would probably have managed to contain it. Such were my thoughts as I raced along. When I got close to the fire I was overwhelmed by the smell of smoke. Roaring flames engulfed the building. My restaurant was burning down. The moment I saw this, my mind went completely blank.

After that, my memory cuts off abruptly. How did I get

home? What did I do when I got back? None of it is clear to me. All I know is that when I snapped out of it, I was home, sitting motionless at the table with my head in my hands. Sleepless nights followed over the next few weeks. I felt so nauseous that I couldn't even eat. If I still had a restaurant, I could work hard to pay back the debts eventually, but with the restaurant burned down, all that was left were those debts.

"What are you going to do, Nobu?" said the voice in my head. "What *can* you do?" said another.

I made up my mind to die, even thought of ways to kill myself—jumping into the cold sea, heading into the mountains with nothing to keep me alive, leaping off a cliff.... Even now, when I recall that period, tears well up in my eyes.

What saved me was my young daughter. She'd climb onto my knees, wanting attention. She was happy that I was finally at home for a while. Looking at her innocent face, I began to think about trying again—if not for my own sake, then at least for hers.

Despair and solitude are twin siblings. When in the depths of despair, people are convinced that they alone are left behind in darkness. But maybe despair feels like darkness only because we keep our eyes tight shut. If we'd only open them, perhaps we'd see that our loved ones are there with us, and that so are other people who depend on us. I believe it is these people who give us the courage to take a step forward and leave despair behind.

When I think about it now, the burning down in one night of my prosperous restaurant—for me, such a painful experience—was a trial set by God. It was a severe trial, to be sure, but God doesn't set problems that are impossible to solve; He only sets ones we can overcome. And to overcome them, we can't keep brooding on them, we have to move forward, taking even one tiny step each day.

My father was a lumber merchant. He died in a traffic accident when I was seven. That morning, he got on his motorcycle and was just about to head for work when I remember asking him to take me with him. "Not today. I'm going somewhere far away," he replied. He really did end up somewhere far away that day.

When I was little, there was a photograph of him I used to look at whenever I felt sad. It was taken on the Pacific island of Palau, where my father had gone to purchase lumber. He is shown with a local of the island under a palm tree. As I stared at this photograph, a resolution began to form in my mind: I too would someday go overseas. Before I knew it, that had become my dream—to work abroad. My father gave me that dream.

After my father died, my older brother took over the lumber job. One day, this brother of mine took me out to eat, probably because he knew I was feeling down. The place he took me to was a sushi restaurant. Until then, I'd never been to one. I followed him in under the curtain leading into the shop, and

a spirited voice burst out: "*Irasshai*! Welcome!" I remember the pleasant smell of vinegar as I entered the restaurant. On the other side of the counter stood the sushi chefs. I admired their brisk movements as they went about making the sushi; I marveled at their sophistication. I wondered, too, about the code-like words they used: *toro* (choice tuna belly), *gyoku* (omelette), *agari* (green tea), *o-aiso* (the check)....

The sushi restaurant my brother took me to offered me my first peep into that grown-up world. I wanted to become a chef myself and make sushi, so striking was the experience of that day.

So, when I graduated from high school, I went on to a live-in job at a sushi restaurant in Shinjuku (Tokyo) called Matsuei. I'd assumed that by getting a job at the restaurant, I would soon be taught how to prepare sushi. I was in for a surprise, however. My job actually entailed shopping for ingredients with the master of the restaurant, carrying things, cleaning the

My father on Palau

place before it opened and serving tea to the customers. There were also odd jobs like delivering food and washing dishes. I am now a chef, but because of my experience as an apprentice, I am able to empathize with waiters and dishwashers.

The master and I would go out to buy fish at the Tsukiji market at six-thirty in the morning, with me carrying a large basket in both hands. The basket was empty on the way there, brimming with fish on the way back. It was so heavy that I sometimes thought my arms would stretch under the weight. So, early in the morning I would be off buying fish; late at night I'd be cleaning and clearing up the restaurant. Sometimes I'd stay until one in the morning. That was my job.

I only had two holidays a month. But since I was putting

away deliveries and clearing up and doing the washing all the time, before I knew it, my day off was coming to a close. And no matter how much time passed, I didn't get to go behind the counter and make sushi. Many times I wondered what on earth I could learn by doing this sort of work. I even thought about giving up. But whenever I felt sick of it all, I'd think about why I chose the job in the first place. I was fixated on the profession of sushi chef as first encountered in the restaurant my brother took me to. I wanted to prepare sushi for customers and watch them smile, knowing they were enjoying the food I'd made for them. It is fantastic making people happy with the food you create.

It would have been easy to quit the restaurant; there were plenty of opportunities to. Yet, no matter how hard I tried to think of other kinds of work I could do, nothing came to mind.

At least, though I wasn't allowed to make sushi yet, I did learn the names of fish and how to judge freshness by going along with the master to the Tsukiji market. Soon I even learned how to select fish according to taste, which of course depends on where it comes from. Before the restaurant opened, I used to watch the master handling fish, and that gave me some idea about how to prepare them.

It was in my third year at Matsuei that I finally got to go behind the counter and actually make sushi. By that time, I had already mastered such basics as how to cut the fish, how to sharpen and handle knives, and how to welcome customers.

At Matsuei Sushi with Mr. Nakane

The joy of creation learned in Peru

One of the regular customers at Matsuei Sushi was a Peruvian of Japanese descent. One day, he suggested with a serious face that I open up a restaurant with him in Peru. I always wanted to have my own place, but I never thought for a minute of opening up in Peru. I didn't know much about the country; I had no idea what sort of fish I could get hold of there or whether I would have access to the ingredients I needed. Also, I wasn't sure whether my food would be well received even if I did open a restaurant there. I decided to go anyway, though, and give it a month of field study.

There were many businesses run by Peruvians of Japanese

descent in the capital city of Lima, where I was planning to open the restaurant. If you drove by car for about twenty minutes, you came to the Pacific Ocean, where sea urchin and abalone abounded. Soon I discovered that the range of fish in Peru was very wide. Japanese food requires fresh fish; Peru was rich in fish, so I decided to make a go of it. I had

At my Peru restaurant

longed to work overseas ever since seeing my father's photograph. Now my dream was fast becoming a reality. I was twenty-four years old and not afraid of anything.

My mother staunchly opposed my going abroad. Stories about Japanese emigrants who'd become destitute in South America made her worried. Maybe she thought I'd never be able to return to Japan if I went. With tears in her eyes, she begged me not to go, did everything she could to stop me. But I wanted to go no matter what. To me, making something from nothing in an unknown country was an attractive prospect. If I hadn't made the decision to leave, I would never have become the man I am today.

Every day in Peru, I went to the local street market to walk around and see what sort of fish had been caught. To me, wondering what sort of fish would be in on any given day was a source of great pleasure. Recipes brewed in my mind.

Not everything that was caught was put on sale at the market. The Peruvians didn't seem to like the look of sea eel and no one ever ate it. Yet sea eel is an indispensable sushi topping. There it lay, unpriced. One day, after buying some other fish, I pointed to the sea eel and said, "I brought my dog over from Japan. He used to eat this every day over there, but now he's lost his pep. I think he misses it." The next day, the fisherman gave me a basket bulging with eel and said, "OK, give this to your dog." I made it into tempura, sushi and the broiled dish called *kabayaki*.

Serving sea eel proved to be lucrative for my restaurant, since no other places were offering it at that time. It so happened that a fellow chef heard about my success and went to buy sea eel for his own restaurant. Apparently he was asked if he, too, had brought his dog over from Japan. Later, when I went back to the market myself, the sea eel was marked with an astonishing price. They had learned that what they'd thought was an unmarketable fish was in fact quite popular in Japan. Seeing my surprise, the man at the stall chuckled and asked how my dog was doing....

There were plenty of fish and vegetables in Peru, but specialized Japanese condiments and processed foods, at least in those days, were scarce. I had no choice but to make from scratch the ingredients I really wanted to use—*kamaboko* (boiled fish paste sausage), *karasumi* (dried mullet roe) and *tonkatsu* (pork cutlet) sauce. I applied myself to the challenge through repeated efforts of trial and error, until finally I was able to produce something I was satisfied with. In this way, I learned to create dishes from scratch.

Chefs have an artistic side to them; they want to make dishes that give people pleasure, not just things that fill the stomach. Because I take pride in my cooking, I don't make any compromises with ingredients, flavorings or presentation. I make only food that I personally am pleased with. For that reason, I select only the freshest fish. I have always been that way. Perhaps that's why, when I was in Peru, the Japanese ambassador, directors of major trading firms and even members of the Japanese imperial family all came to my restaurant. I had a good reputation, and business boomed. All was well in Peru. I lived in a palatial residence, complete with a gardener and maid. I had a daughter with my wife, whom I'd married before coming to Peru. There were no problems at all, except one: the differences I had with my business partner.

In Peru with my wife Yoko and oldest daughter

What concerned me most was making food I was happy with. This meant high-quality food, made from excellent ingredients. This was my priority as a chef. But all my partner thought about was profit. He told me that our food costs were too high and asked me to use cheaper ingredients. We talked things over many times, but his priority was always "the bottom line." My pride wouldn't allow me to lower my standards. So, after three years of work in Peru, I withdrew from the restaurant entirely.

I benefited greatly from working in Peru. The experience of making unavailable ingredients and flavorings from scratch gave me a lot of confidence. While I lived there, I reworked home-style Peruvian dishes and made my own version of *anticucho*, a local snack served at concession stands. These concoctions later became part of my repertoire.

From Argentina to Alaska to LA

After I quit the restaurant in Peru, I went to work at a Japanese restaurant in the capital of Argentina, Buenos Aires. This was a restaurant that an acquaintance had introduced me to. Buenos Aires, the "Paris of South America," is a beautiful city where prices are remarkably cheap. But the staple in that country is meat, and even the restaurant where I worked mainly served meat items like *sukiyaki* and *shabu-shabu*. Without fish, I couldn't demonstrate my true abilities. In fact, I felt a lot like a fish out of water myself, so to speak. Moreover, because of the low labor wages in Argentina, the money I had saved up until then quickly began to disappear. I panicked when I thought I might have to spend the rest of my life there.

I didn't think Argentina was the right place for me to work. I had only been in the country for a year, but because I was unable to do what I wanted, the days seemed to drag on endlessly. I knew I couldn't go on like this. Ultimately, after four years, I brought my life in South America to an end and decided to go home.

Japan has the greatest wealth of food anywhere. Even much of the seafood there is imported from all over the world. There are as many Japanese restaurants in the country as there are stars in the sky, but going back to work at one was not easy. I had been virtually my own boss for four years in South America and I couldn't bear to work for someone else again. I also felt I had come back from South America defeated and wanted another shot at working overseas.

It was at about this time that someone approached me and asked if I was interested in going into business together in Alaska. The idea of opening a restaurant in Alaska appealed to me, so I made up my mind to go.

I had been full of dreams when I first set out for Peru, but heading for Alaska I had even greater aspirations. That's why, when my restaurant burned down, I felt as if all my hopes and ambitions had gone up in smoke with it.

On the advice of a friend, I later moved to Los Angeles and began working at a sushi bar. This time I wasn't starting from zero, but from below zero, saddled with debts. When I opened Matsuhisa in Los Angeles, it was nine years after what had happened in Alaska.

From the outset, I was determined to make Matsuhisa a place where I could create my ideal cuisine. I didn't skimp on buying good fish, so food costs always ran high. The restaurant was sure to get support, I was convinced, if only I used good ingredients and put my heart into making good food. Making no profit was OK, I thought, so long as my customers were satisfied. I myself managed to get by and I could pay my staff and the people I worked with. With my Beverly Hills restaurant, I was determined to realize the dreams that had ended as mere good intentions at my place in Peru.

When the restaurant opened I didn't do any fancy advertising, nor did I even want to. As I went on, though, always striving for high quality and service, Matsuhisa built up a reputation for excellent food and for serving unusual dishes.

Customers who had come once brought along their friends the next time around, and those friends, in turn, then brought their friends. In this way, before a year had passed, the restaurant was full every day.

In the second year after opening, we were awarded three stars as "Best Japanese Restaurant"' by the Californian Press Association, and also came out top in the general category in a Zagat Restaurant Survey popularity vote. In addition, we were chosen by *The New York Times* as one of its top ten world restaurants, and I personally was selected as one of America's top ten chefs by *Food & Wine* Magazine. I think it is safe to say that I completed the assignment that God had set me.

Matsuhisa has been visited by countless Hollywood stars, including Tom Cruise, Richard Gere and Madonna. Robert De Niro likewise had been coming since we first opened. It was he who asked me, after only a year of being in business, to open another restaurant with him in New York. He even invited me to New York to show me around a building he'd bought.

"This can be the restaurant. Here's the party room. And I'm thinking of making this the screening room," he explained as we went up and down in the elevator. I felt his enthusiasm, but deep down I was scared about starting up a new restaurant after what had happened in Alaska. What's more, I had my hands full with Matsuhisa. So I was wary, and after agonizing over it for some time, I finally turned him down. De Niro thought about it a bit and said OK, he understood. Afterward, whenever he was in Los Angeles, he'd drop in to the restaurant and ask me how I was doing.

One day, about four years later, I received a phone call at my house. It was from De Niro. When I picked up the phone, he said abruptly, "So Nobu, how about it?" For a minute I didn't know what he meant. I had no idea he was still thinking of opening a New York Matsuhisa after I'd refused. He said that he'd found another good location. For four years he had watched me at work, patiently waiting until I felt ready to expand my business. I was moved by his determination.

And so Nobu New York, my joint project with Robert De Niro, opened in Manhattan. The concept was the same as Matsuhisa, and it was soon well on its way to being my ideal restaurant. The food itself had an impact, as did the service.

Working in LA before Matsuhisa

Inside, it was a lively scene. You could always sense the care taken by each and every staff member. We served delicious dishes without setting limits on food costs. Above all, though, people loved it. I don't for a minute regret the effort I put into making both Matsuhisa and Nobu what they are today, and just pray they stay that way.

My food, Nobu style

I believe food is culture, as well as fashion. When delicious new recipes are developed, they tend to spread globally. The Soft Shell Crab Roll (page 160) on the menu of Matsuhisa and Nobu is one such recipe. Soft shell crab is best eaten fried in oil. I experimented with different cooking methods, but found that frying was the best. I'd served soft shell crab at my restaurants before, but I never made a roll out of it until a customer one day asked me to. As a chef, I take my customers' whims seriously, so I tried making a roll, using the usual vinegared rice and *nori*. I quickly became convinced of its potential. Then I considered how to serve it; rolling it in vinegared rice alone was uninteresting, so I added avocado, flying fish roe, *asatsuki* chives and sesame seeds. Then I rolled up these ingredients in vinegared rice. Finally I wrapped one long, thin strip of cucumber around the outside. The lovely translucent green gave it a fresh feeling, while the taste and texture of the hot soft-shell crab and the bursting crunch of the flying fish roe and sesame seeds on the inside made for an interesting combination of flavors.

New Style Sashimi (page 116) is another dish that came about as a result of a customer's request. I had gotten hold of some fresh flounder, so I cut it into paper-thin slices and served it raw. But the dish came back to the kitchen because the customer couldn't eat fish that hadn't been cooked. I wanted to somehow utilize the fish I'd so carefully and elaborately arranged. So I looked about the kitchen for an idea. My gaze fell upon some olive oil that had been heated in a frying pan. "That's it," I thought. Sesame oil would be combined with heated olive oil to add aroma. The raw fish would be topped with ginger spears and *menegi* and then drizzled with *ponzu*. Then the hot oil would be poured over it. The customer who had claimed not to be able to eat raw fish understood the way I felt and tried a mouthful, then two, and ended up leaving the plate clean.

I am supremely happy at times like these. There is no greater compliment to a chef's skills than to be able to make a diner enjoy something he or she couldn't eat before.

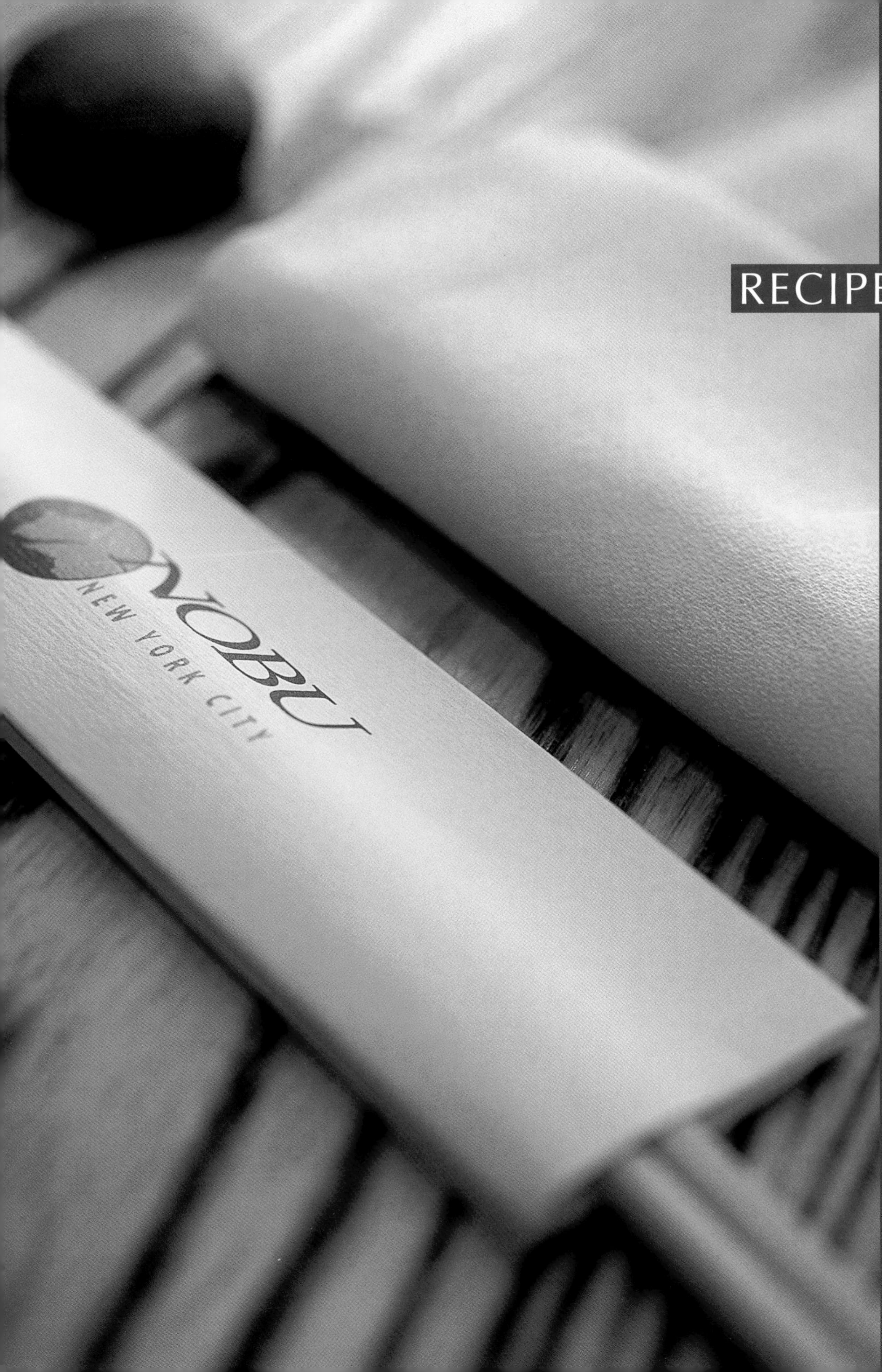

RECIPES

INGREDIENTS, TECHNIQUES, EQUIPMENT AND MEASUREMENTS

INGREDIENTS

Many of the recipes here involve unfamiliar Japanese ingredients with difficult-sounding names. Most of these ingredients, however, are sold outside Japan at specialist supermarkets, some of which are listed in the section on suppliers at the back of this book. The glossary also provides succinct explanations of all the Japanese ingredients and some of the more esoteric Western ingredients used.

Seafood

I have always worked with seafood and can tell at a glance how fresh something is, but I still benefit from the tips a good fishmonger can pass on. So my advice to less experienced cooks is to cultivate a good relationship with your fishmonger, who will know what is in season and what is the best buy of the day. If requested, he may also filet and clean the seafood, which is particularly recommended for trickier sea creatures like octopus, cuttlefish and squid.

Sea Salt

Never use too much salt because it will overwhelm the flavor of your cooking. When added gradually and carefully, the right amount can make an impact on the overall taste of a dish and sometimes bring out the more subtle, and often hidden, flavors.

Soy Sauce

This pungent, brown salty sauce is, of course, one of the primary seasonings of Japanese cooking. Light soy sauce is amber in color, clearer and thinner, yet saltier than standard soy sauce. Used in smaller quantities than standard soy sauce, it doesn't darken the color of the food. Low sodium soy sauces are also now available for people who have to restrict their daily sodium intake. I only use it in Wasabi Pepper Sauce (page 173) because other soy sauces would overwhelm the flavors of the other ingredients.

Saké

Amino acids in saké make this rice wine an excellent food tenderizer. Saké also acts to suppress saltiness and prevent delicate flavors from expiring. If you object to the smell of alcohol, use Nikiri Zaké (page 174). Saké should never play the leading role in flavoring; *mirin* and saké are merely supporting players.

Mirin

This sweet liquid flavoring containing 14% alcohol is used exclusively in cooking to add a mild sweetness and to glaze grilled food when used in a basting sauce. Its sweetness is very different from sugar.

Bonito Flakes

The Japanese have been eating the bonito, a member of the mackerel family, since as long ago as the eighth century and using dried bonito flakes since the fifteenth century. Bonito fillets are steamed, dried, smoked and cured until they become as hard as wood. The whole process takes as long as six months. The "petrified" fillets are shaved into flakes and used as one of the two essential ingredients (the other is *konbu*) of *dashi*, the basic soup stock of Japanese cooking. *Dashi* always tastes best when made with just-shaved flakes. A special shaver called a *katsuo-kezuri-ki* ("bonito shaver") is used, resembling a carpenter's plane fixed above a single-drawer box, and producing flakes that look like pinkish-tan curls. Commercially prepared and packaged flakes are also available and make good stock. The size of the flakes depends somewhat on the bonito shaver or the brand of packaged flakes. For this reason, it is not really possible to measure bonito flakes in terms of cups, tablespoons or teaspoons. In this cookbook I have expressed the amount used in ounces and grams.

Konbu

Konbu is a variety of kelp that grows in the cold seas off the coast of Hokkaido. From July to September, live *konbu* is harvested in special boats and brought to the shore where it is dried, first in the sun, and then by hot-air fans in special drying chambers. The dried *konbu* is then allowed to mature for two years before being folded into bundles and sent to market. Rich in monosodium glu-

tamate, the *konbu* sold in supermarkets as *dashikonbu* in fairly large pieces is used for making *dashi*. This *konbu* should never be washed because the flavor lies on the surface. At most, wipe it clean with a cloth and remove it from the *dashi* before the water comes to a boil to prevent scum from forming on the surface.

Miso

This fermented paste of soybeans and either rice or barley with salt is an essential ingredient in the Japanese larder. Most Japanese will associate it with *miso* soup, where it is combined with *dashi*. Indeed, I remember the *miso* soup that my mother made for me each morning as the first taste that taught me how delicious Japanese food can be. *Miso*, however, is used in other ways too. It may be thinned and used as dressing; left in its thick state as a pickling medium; or spread on grilled foods.

There are many different kinds of *miso*, each with its own aroma, flavor, color and texture. Yet they are all made by essentially the same process: crushing boiled soybeans and adding barley or rice, then injecting the mixture with a yeastlike mold. The mixture is left to mature for anything from a couple of months to three years. Three types of *miso* are used in this cookbook. Red *miso*, Japan's most popular rice *miso*, is salty and rich in protein. White *miso*, on the other hand, is rather sweet. Made from fermented barley, *moromi miso* is never used for making *miso* soup. This soft, dark brown paste is most often eaten with chilled cucumber.

Oils

The best oils for deep-frying are the highly refined, pale golden ones that are a blend of various vegetable products—soybean oil, vegetable oil, rapeseed oil, palm oil and coconut oil. Although tasteless, they are recommended for frying because of their high smoke point.

For New Style Oil, which is heated until it is very hot, I use a combination of pure olive and sesame oils. Pure olive oil is refined and therefore isn't as heavy as extra virgin olive oil, in addition to having a higher smoke point. Aromatic sesame oil adds an Asian accent to New Style Oil and other sauces and dressings.

Along with extra virgin olive, I also use grapeseed oil in my sauces and dressings. Low in cholesterol, this light, aromatic oil is a by-product of the wine industry and popular in France and Italy. Unlike other oils, grapeseed oil will not solidify when left in the refrigerator—an important consideration when making sauces and dressings that won't be used up immediately.

Garnishes

Garnishes are used to provide a dish with an accent of color, texture or flavor. In many cases, a single green leaf is all that is needed to turn a dish into a visual delight. Seasonal flowers, leaves and plants will all add a sense of season to your food. I have used many garnishes in the recipes in this book, most of which are only available in Japan. Don't worry, as they are all optional. Look around—perhaps in your garden—for seasonal flowers, leaves and vegetables that you can use to express your own sensibility and your feelings about the season.

CUTTING TECHNIQUES

There are three basic Japanese cutting techniques used in this book.

Usu-zukuri

This method of cutting thin slices is most appropriate for firm white fish, such as red snapper, sea bass and flounder. Place the fillet horizontally on a chopping board with the skin side up and the tail end on the left, steadying this end with the fingers of your left hand. Hold the knife so that the top is inclined sharply to the right and, from the left of the fillet, start cutting paper-thin slices, keeping the blade at an acute angle to achieve a clean cut across the grain. The fish is sliced in one drawing stroke. Let the weight of the knife do the work as you draw the blade back.

Ha-uchi

This method of making small cuts or incisions is useful for improving the texture of tough seafood, such as abalone, ark shell, octopus and squid. Hold the knife at an angle of forty-five degrees from the upright position, so that the heel of the blade is pointing downward. Lightly tap with the heel to score lines on the surface of the seafood without cutting all the way through.

Good sushi chefs will always employ the *ha-uchi* technique on tough, chewy sushi toppings to ensure better adhesion with the sushi rice, otherwise the rice will break away from the topping when the sushi is eaten.

The *ha-uchi* technique is also used to prevent shrimp from curling during cooking.

Katsura-muki

This method of cutting a piece of fruit or a vegetable to reduce it to one long, unbroken peel is used for making shredded *daikon*, *udo* curls and carrot curls. Holding a knife firmly, move the fruit or vegetable against the knife, turning it gradually to cut the flesh into a thin, ribbonlike strip.

Knives

A sashimi slicer (*sashimi-bocho*) is particularly recommended for both the *usu-zukuri* and *katsura-muki* cutting techniques. This long, thin-bladed, pointed knife is known as a "willow-leaf blade" (*yanagi-bocho*).

A kitchen cleaver (*deba-bocho*) is a versatile fish knife used for fileting fish, among other things. It may seem thick and heavy at first, but you will soon find that it's effective at delicate kitchen work too.

Make sure that you keep your knives in good condition with a clean, sharp cutting edge. Unless the blade is very sharp, both the *usu-zukuri* and *katsura-muki* techniques will be very difficult.

The *ha-uchi* cutting technique can be done with the heel of any good kitchen knife.

EQUIPMENT

There are very few references made to special utensils or equipment in this book. A well-equipped Western kitchen is perfectly adequate for making most of the recipes presented here. The four pieces of equipment listed below are not essential, but they will make lighter work of some of the recipes. They can all be bought from oriental goods stores.

Bamboo Rolling Mat

Called a *makisu* in Japanese, a bamboo rolling mat is used to compress soft materials into cylindrical forms, as with Monkfish Pâté with Caviar and Mustard Su-miso Sauce (page 98) and Sea Eel Dragon Roll (page 164). A standard mat is about 9 inches by 9½ inches (23cm x 24cm) and is made by weaving together thin bamboo strips with strong cotton string.

Remember to wash the mat with tepid running water after use. Wipe the mat dry with a cloth and leave it to dry completely before putting it away in order to avoid musty smells.

Grater

Called an *oroshigane*, a Japanese grater for ginger or *wasabi* will grate more finely than most Western graters. Usually, a home grater is made of stainless steel, aluminum or plastic and has a flat surface textured with raised spikes. A cheese grater will work just as well as an *oroshigane*. Use either when the recipe calls for "finely grated ginger" or "finely grated garlic." Spiny Lobster Soup (page 58) requires the juice from grated ginger, so either grate onto cheesecloth or squeeze out the juice with your hands.

Make sure that nothing remains between the spikes when you wash the grater.

Ceramic Mortar

A ceramic mortar (*suribachi*) and wooden pestle (*surikogi*) are designed to crush and

grind seeds and leaves into a paste. The inside of the mortar is unglazed and textured with a comb pattern, while the outside is smooth and glazed, usually in brown. The *suribachi*'s textured interior acts like a grater against the seeds and leaves. Use a pestle and mortar to make Kuruma Shrimp Filo with Cilantro Sauce (page 56), Fairy Squid with Kinome Su-miso Sauce (page 90) and Aji Panca Sauce (page 170). A ceramic mortar is also essential for removing the sliminess from an octopus (page 68).

Wash the mortar with water and a stiff brush. The tip of a bamboo skewer will sometimes help loosen any bits that have become stuck in the grooves.

Automatic Rice Cooker

No Japanese kitchen is complete without an automatic rice cooker. Cooking rice in a saucepan over the stove takes practice, time and skill to get right. More importantly, the cook has to be there while the rice is cooking. With an automatic rice cooker, one simply supplies the right amounts of washed rice and water and pushes a switch to start the cooking process. The rice cooker will even switch to a keep-warm function when the rice is done. For perfect results every time, invest in one to make Black Rice-Stuffed Squid (page 86) and Vinegared Sushi Rice (page 158).

Wash the nonstick cooking pot in warm water. Wipe the other parts of the automatic rice cooker with a damp cloth.

MEASUREMENTS

All measurements (capacity, weight, length and temperature) are shown in both American and metric units in this book. Ingredients were originally measured out in metric units, which are used by my restaurants in Japan and Europe. The American units quoted, then, are approximate equivalents based on the tables listed below.

Capacity

The cup used in this cookbook refers to the standard Japanese cup and *not* the American one. The Japanese cup is about 5/6 of an American cup or 6 4/5 fluid ounces (200ml), and more useful when measuring Japanese ingredients, particularly when making rice. A metric equivalent, in either milliliters or grams, is always provided in parentheses after a cup measurement. Teaspoons and tablespoons are the standard sizes.

1 teaspoon = 1/16 fluid ounce = 5ml	1/4 cup = 3 tablespoons plus 1 teaspoon = 50ml	Quarts and liters are almost the same.
1 tablespoon = 1/2 fluid ounce = 15ml	1/2 cup = 7 tablespoons plus 1 teaspoon = 100ml	
	3/4 cup = 10 tablespoons = 150ml	
	1 cup = 13 tablespoons plus 1 teaspoon = 200ml	

Weights

grams × 0.035 = ounces
ounces × 28.35 = grams

APPROXIMATE EQUIVALENTS:

1/8 ounce = 4g	2 ounces = 60g	8 1/2 ounces = 240g
1/3 ounce = 10g	3 1/2 ounces = 100g	9 ounces = 250g
1/2 ounce = 15g	4 1/4 ounces = 120g	14 ounces = 400g
2/3 ounce = 20g	5 1/4 ounces = 150g	18 ounces = 500g
1 ounce = 30g	6 1/2 ounces = 180g	2 1/4 pounds = 1kg
1 1/2 ounces = 40g	7 ounces = 200g	
1 3/4 ounces = 50g	1/2 pound = 8 ounces = 230g	

Lengths

inches × 0.39 = centimeters
centimeters × 2.54 = inches

APPROXIMATE EQUIVALENTS:

1/16 inch = 2mm	3/8 inch = 1cm	2 inches = 5cm
1/8 inch = 4mm	1 inch = 2.5cm	3 inches = 8cm

SHELLFISH

ABALONE

Unlike in Japan—where abalone enjoys the cachet of being an expensive delicacy—many Americans find this admittedly bland-tasting shellfish chewy and hard when served as sushi or sashimi. The onus is definitely on the chef to conjure up recipes with enough creativity and imagination to entice the customer to choose an abalone dish from the menu. While abalone is found in the seas around the United States, recent over-fishing of impressive specimens in Californian waters has led to a total ban on all catches of this shellfish for the foreseeable future. Fortunately, abalone is now commercially farmed in California.

There are two quite different ways of preparing abalone so that it is neither hard nor chewy: either cook it very briefly or cook it very slowly. Reflecting my personal preference for barely cooked abalone, I have included two unique recipes in which the abalone is exposed to heat for only a few seconds. Inspired by Japanese *somen* noodles, Abalone Somen (page 24) is a light, summery preparation refreshingly served over crushed ice. The hard, usually inedible outer bits of the abalone are grilled, diced and served with a chilled dipping sauce for added bite. Based on a similar concept, but with a different sauce, Abalone Shabu-shabu with Egg Sauce and Caviar (page 30) is a dynamic combination of blanched abalone slices, egg sauce and caviar.

For Steamed Abalone with Mustard Su-miso Sauce and Junsai (page 28), the abalone is steamed in *dashi* and saké for thirty minutes to soften the flesh. The more traditional *saka-mushi* found in sushi restaurants is made by steaming the abalone with saké, *daikon* rounds and salt for six or seven hours. I make my version more quickly in a pressure cooker for a more concentrated, richer flavor.

PREPARING ABALONE

1. To remove the abalone meat from its shell: Slide a metal spatula, or some other thin, flat tool, under the meat and along the inside of the shell. Pull the meat away from the shell.

2. Cut away the liver and the radula (hard, projecting black edge) from the meat.

3. Salt the meat. Scrub the abalone well in cold water with a brush to remove dirt and debris.

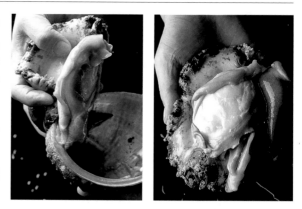

SCALLOPS

Scallops are a familiar ingredient in many cuisines, not just Japanese. Although soft when eaten raw, perhaps because the scallop is actually a muscle it develops a certain chewy resistance when exposed to a little heat. I love them either way and am equally fond of dried scallops, which make wonderful *dashi* when reconstituted with water.

Scallops with Creamy Spicy Sauce (page 36) is without doubt the single most popular scallop dish on my menu. Like so many of my original creations, this recipe came about almost by accident. The first time I made it, I was simply going to salamander some leftover scraps of scallop and surf clams on their shells. It was then that I thought of mayonnaise. Coated in mayonnaise, the scallops and clams were browned beautifully. The taste intrigued me: rich and gratin-like—even better when Chinese chili bean sauce or *wasabi* or even *miso* was added to the mayonnaise. For an "explosive" surprise, try our special "dynamite" version of this sauce: Finely chopped onion adds volume to the mayonnaise, which melts as the scallops are being broiled.

Most of my cooking combines seafood and vegetables: Grilled Scallops with Tabbouleh Salsa (page 34) is no exception. Japanese cooks usually grill scallops on a wire grill and serve them with soy sauce and lemon. But I enjoy pairing different flavors for new tastes, one reason why I serve scallops with various vegetable mixtures and match hot food with cold salsas.

OYSTERS

It fascinates me to think that although sashimi is the quintessential Japanese food, raw oysters—particularly when served on the half shell—are more typical of European and American cuisines. Oysters are eaten raw in Japan as well as put in stews and deep-fried, but they are not commonly eaten in summer. Outside Japan, of course, a rich variety of oysters is enjoyed all the year around. My ceviche (page 118), tiradito (pages 74 and 120) and New Style Sashimi (page 116) are excellent with oysters. I also serve them simply topped with caviar and sprinkled with lemon juice, or sometimes in the Japanese way with *ponzu* (page 174). My personal favorite is raw oysters with sea salt, black pepper and lemon juice.

ABALONE SOMEN

The REFRESHING appearance of this dish is ideal for SUMMER. The FLESHY parts around the ABALONE "foot" are seared and served as a FLAVORFUL accompaniment along with scallions and grated ginger.

INGREDIENTS — serves 4

Dipping Sauce

¾ cup (150ml) Dashi (page 174)

1 tablespoon plus 2 teaspoons *mirin*

1 tablespoon plus 2 teaspoons soy sauce

• • •

1 ½ ounces (40g) white scallions (spring onions), finely sliced

1 abalone in the shell, about 1 pound (500g), removed and cleaned (page 22)

sea salt

½ cup (50g) potato flour

10 *shiso* leaves, finely shredded

hoba magnolia leaves for garnish, optional

dogtooth violet for garnish, optional

1 teaspoon finely grated ginger

METHOD

1. Make the dipping sauce: Bring the *dashi* to a boil in a small saucepan over low heat. Add the *mirin* and soy sauce, and then turn off the heat. Leave to cool.

2. Soak the finely sliced scallions in cold water for 5 minutes to remove any astringency and drain.

3. Lay the prepared abalone cup side down and cut away the hard projecting black sections around the edge. Season these cut-away parts with a little sea salt and grill on high heat. Chop into small chunks, no more than ⅛ inch (5mm) square. These will be used later as a condiment.

4. Insert a knife sideways into the white foot of the abalone and slice as thinly as possible, about 1/16 inch (2mm) thick. Then cut the slices into fine strips no more than ⅛ inch (5mm) wide.

5. Dust the abalone strips with potato flour and lightly shake off the excess.

6. Have ready a medium saucepan of boiling water and a bowl of iced water. Add a pinch of sea salt to the boiling water and dip the abalone strips in it for 5 to 6 seconds. An attractive semi-translucent film will form over the abalone when the potato flour is cooked through. Remove the abalone strips from the boiling water, plunge briefly into the iced water and drain in a colander.

7. Arrange the abalone strips over crushed ice on a serving dish lined with some *hoba* magnolia leaves. Heap the shredded *shiso* leaves alongside and garnish with dogtooth violet. Serve with the dipping sauce and small dishes containing the chopped scallions, grated ginger and previously grilled abalone chunks.

I USE THE SAME CONDIMENTS usually served with *somen* in Japan. Dip the abalone strips into the cold sauce and eat with chopped scallions, grated ginger or the grilled abalone chunks.

"*SOMEN* ARE VERY FINE,

WHITE NOODLES TRADITIONALLY EATEN CHILLED WITH A COLD DIPPING SAUCE DURING THE SUMMER. The difference between *somen* and other Japanese noodles lies in the way they are made. Whereas all other noodles are made by rolling out dough and cutting it into thin strips, *somen* are made by pulling the dough. To make *somen*, wheat flour is mixed with salt and water and kneaded by hand. After being flattened into a long, flat belt, the dough is pulled gradually at intervals, to give it time to rest and "mature." Finally, when the dough is as thin as vermicelli, it is dried in the sun. Fresh squid can also be finely sliced and served in the same way: This is called *ika somen* (squid *somen*)."

ABALONE WITH WASABI PEPPER SAUCE

THE MILD FLAVOR OF ABALONE IS JOINED BY THE PIQUANCY OF *WASABI* AND *SHICHIMI TOGARASHI*. THE THIN SLICES OF ABALONE ARE SWIFTLY ADDED TO THE SAUCE WHEN JUST COOKED.

INGREDIENTS ———————————————————————————— serves 4

1 abalone in the shell, about 1 pound (500g), removed and cleaned (page 22)

½ cup (100ml) clarified butter (page 173)

1 clove garlic, thinly sliced

4 spears green asparagus, cut into 2-inch (5-cm) lengths

4 spears white asparagus, cut into 2-inch (5-cm) lengths

7 ounces (200g) of at least three varieties of mushroom (*shiitake, yanagi matsutake, pied bleu* and *enoki* used here), cut into bite-size pieces

sea salt

freshly ground black pepper

shichimi togarashi to taste

¾ cup (150ml) Wasabi Pepper Sauce (page 173)

shredded and fried beet (beetroot) for garnish

METHOD

1. Cut the prepared abalone into very thin slices, about 1/16 inch (2mm) thick.

2. Place a medium frying pan over medium heat, then add the clarified butter and the garlic. When the aroma of the garlic is released, turn the heat up to high, add the asparagus and mushrooms and sauté. Sprinkle with a little sea salt, black pepper and *shichimi togarashi*.

3. Add the abalone slices to the frying pan. Sauté briefly and then add the Wasabi Pepper Sauce. Remove from heat.

4. Transfer to a serving dish and garnish with beet shreds.

THIS DISH SHOULD BE PUT TOGETHER with speed so the flavors of all the ingredients harmonize in an instant. If the abalone is cooked too long, it will toughen and shrivel.

STEAMED ABALONE WITH MUSTARD SU-MISO SAUCE AND JUNSAI

APPRECIATE THE SWEETNESS AND TEXTURE OF SLOW-COOKED ABALONE. TO PAIR EARLY SUMMER *JUNSAI* WITH SUMMER ABALONE IS TO FEAST ON THE SEASON ITSELF.

INGREDIENTS

serves 4

5 cups (1l) Dashi (page 174)

1 tablespoon light soy sauce

3 tablespoons saké

½ teaspoon sea salt

1 ounce (30g) peeled *daikon*

1 abalone in the shell, about 1 pound (500g), removed and cleaned (page 22)

1 cup (200ml) Mustard Su-miso Sauce (page 172)

3 ½ ounces (100g) *junsai*, optional

⅔ ounce (20g) fresh truffles, finely sliced into thin strips

METHOD

1. Place the *dashi*, soy sauce, saké, sea salt and *daikon* in a pressure cooker. Add the abalone, cover and set on high heat. When steam emerges, turn the heat down to low and simmer for 30 minutes.

2. After the pressure cooker has cooled, take off the lid, remove the abalone and cut it into ⅛-inch- (5-mm-) thick slices.

3. Line a serving dish with the Mustard Su-miso Sauce, arrange the abalone on top and scatter the *junsai* around the abalone. Garnish with the truffles.

IN JAPANESE COOKING, *daikon* is added to the pot when stewing shellfish and octopus, as it is said to have tenderizing qualities.

"RELATED TO THE WATER LILY, *JUNSAI,* OR WATER SHIELD, IS AN EARLY SUMMER AQUATIC PLANT with mild-flavored, edible leaves and buds. It is instantly recognizable to Japanese as summer food."

ABALONE SHABU-SHABU WITH EGG SAUCE AND CAVIAR

PAPER-THIN SLICES OF ABALONE ARE BLANCHED BRIEFLY IN BOILING WATER, PLUNGED INTO ICED WATER, THEN SERVED WITH A CAVIAR-LADEN EGG SAUCE.

INGREDIENTS ———————————————————————————— serves 4

1 abalone in the shell, about 1 pound (500g), removed and cleaned (page 22)

sea salt

fresh seaweed

Egg Sauce (use 4 egg yolks: page 170)

2 ½ tablespoons caviar

shredded *daikon* for garnish (page 174), optional

carrot curls for garnish (page 174), optional

shiso buds for garnish, optional

METHOD

1. Cut the abalone into very thin slices, about ¹/₁₆ inch (2 mm) thick.

2. Add a pinch of salt to a large pot of boiling water. Immerse the abalone slices in the boiling water for 5 seconds. Remove and plunge into iced water briefly. Drain in a colander.

3. Line the abalone shell with the seaweed and top with the abalone slices. You might put the Egg Sauce (with caviar added) in an ear shell—we like to call it "baby abalone" in my restaurants—or any other small shell. Garnish with shredded *daikon*, carrot curls and *shiso* buds.

THE SAUCE FROM THE RECIPE for Octopus Shabu-shabu with Spicy Ume Sauce (page 76) also works well in this dish instead of the egg sauce.

"SHABU-SHABU IS A ONE-POT DISH IN WHICH *DASHI* OR WATER IS HEATED IN A PAN and very thinly sliced fresh beef or pork is dipped in to cook for several seconds. The cooked slices are then dipped in an accompanying sauce. I also make *shabu-shabu* with octopus (page 76) and *toro*."

SCALLOP FILO WITH TRUFFLE YUZU SAUCE

CRISP FILO CONTRASTS WITH THE SLIGHTLY CHEWY TEXTURE OF THE SCALLOP.
EAT THE SCALLOPS IN ONE MOUTHFUL WITH PLENTY OF SAUCE.

INGREDIENTS ———————————————————— serves 4

Truffle *yuzu* sauce

1 3/4 ounces (50g) fresh truffles

8 tablespoons Yuzu Dressing (page 173)

4 scallops in the shell

Tempura Batter (page 174)

3 1/2 ounces (100g) shredded filo (page 56)

vegetable oil for deep-frying

hamabofu for garnish, optional

METHOD

1. Make the sauce: Add the truffles to the Yuzu Dressing and blend in a food processor for about 10 seconds, or until the truffles are finely ground.

2. Extract the scallops from their shells, remove and reserve the beard (the surrounding muscle flap) and discard the innards. Rinse the foot—the central adductor muscle commonly referred to as the scallop when shelled—in cold water and drain.

3. Dip the scallops in the tempura batter and then wrap in the filo. Make sure the whole scallop is wrapped by rotating it 4 or 5 times in different directions. Filo dries out easily, so sandwich the scallops between dampened sheets of paper towels after wrapping them.

4. Bring about 3 inches (8cm) of oil in a medium saucepan to 340°F (170°C). Deep-fry the scallops for 3 to 4 minutes. Also fry the reserved beard. Drain on paper towels.

5. Line the scallop shells with the sauce. Add the scallops and top with scraps of beard as decoration. Garnish with *hamabofu*.

"THE USE OF *HAMABOFU*, A COASTAL PLANT, IN COOKING IS UNIQUE TO JAPAN: Since olden times the young leaves of this early spring plant have been used for boiled vegetable dishes like *o-hitashi* and *aemono*, and the roots pickled."

I THINK ANY SAUCE IS A GOOD MATCH for fried food. I like to serve hot, just-cooked foods with cold salsas as well—for example this dish would also be good served with Maui Onion Salsa (page 171) or Matsuhisa Salsa (page 171).

GRILLED SCALLOPS WITH TABBOULEH SALSA

PLUMP SCALLOPS, SPRINKLED WITH SALT AND PEPPER, ARE LIGHTLY GRILLED AND SERVED WITH A SALSA RICH IN PARSLEY AND DICED VEGETABLES.

INGREDIENTS ———————————————————————————— serves 4

8 scallops in the shell

sea salt

freshly ground black pepper

4 cups (800ml) Tabbouleh Salsa (page 172)

cucumber flowers for garnish, optional

METHOD

1. Extract the scallops from their shells. Remove the beard and the innards and discard. Rinse the scallops in cold water and drain.

2. Preheat a grill or broiler to high. Season both sides of the scallops with a little sea salt and black pepper. Grill the scallops on a wire rack until the surfaces are just brown.

3. Place the Tabbouleh Salsa on a serving plate and arrange the scallops. Garnish with a cucumber flower.

I LIKE TO PUT SO MUCH PARSLEY in the salsa that it looks almost completely green. This salsa should be made just before eating; otherwise the liquid content of the vegetables will turn the dish watery.

"I FIRST ENCOUNTERED TABBOULEH IN ISRAEL. The traditional Middle Eastern salad was made with bulgur, cucumber, tomato, mint and parsley."

SCALLOPS WITH CREAMY SPICY SAUCE

Fresh scallops are SLATHERED with a PIQUANT mayonnaise and baked. The golden brown MAYONNAISE topping blankets the SNAP of flying fish roe, *enoki* mushrooms and fresh *nori*.

INGREDIENTS ———————————————————————————— serves 4

4 scallops in the shell

7 ounces (200g) *enoki* mushrooms

4 tablespoons flying fish roe

4 teaspoons shredded fresh *nori*

5 tablespoons plus 1 teaspoon Creamy Spicy Sauce (page 170)

fresh seaweed for garnish

2 limes, halved

METHOD

1. Preheat the oven to 475°F (250°C, gas 9).

2. Extract the scallops from their shells. Remove the beard and innards and discard. Rinse the scallops in cold water and drain. Reserve shells and scrub thoroughly. Cut each scallop into 4 pieces of equal size.

3. Preheat a grill or broiler. Spread the mushrooms over the insides of the reserved shells. Layer the scallop pieces over the mushrooms and bake for 3 to 4 minutes. Remove the scallops from the oven and top with flying fish roe, fresh *nori* and finally the Creamy Spicy Sauce. Grill or broil until the surface turns golden brown.

4. Arrange the scallop shells on a seaweed-lined plate. Serve with halved limes.

TRY COMBINING THE MAYONNAISE with *wasabi*, Japanese mustard or *miso* instead of chili garlic sauce.

OYSTERS WITH NOBU'S THREE SALSAS

SAVOR RAW OYSTERS SERVED WITH THREE SPICY, SLIGHTLY SWEET AND FIERY SALSAS.

INGREDIENTS ── serves 4

12 fresh oysters in the shell

4 tablespoons Matsuhisa Salsa (page 171)

4 tablespoons Maui Onion Salsa (page 171)

4 tablespoons Jalapeño Salsa (page 171)

finely chopped chives for garnish

METHOD

1. Remove the oysters from their shells and rinse under cold water. Drain.

2. Arrange the oysters in their shells on a serving dish lined with crushed ice and top with a little of each salsa—i.e. four oysters per salsa.

3. Sprinkle the chives over the Maui Onion Salsa.

THIS TRIO OF SALSAS IS ALSO A GOOD MATCH with mussels boiled in salted water. In Peru, *choros con salsa criolla* are mussels sprinkled with ingredients like onion, cilantro (coriander), chili paste and lemon juice.

"A REGULAR MATSUHISA CUSTOMER ONCE ASKED ME TO HIDE A DIAMOND ENGAGE-MENT RING IN AN OYSTER AS HE WANTED TO SURPRISE HIS GIRLFRIEND, AN OYSTER AFICIONADO. When she arrived, I poured them some champagne and served Oysters with Nobu's Three Salsas. We watched with bated breath as she ate first one oyster, then another. Finally she gasped when she saw the ring under the third. Falling down on one knee, he lost no time with his proposal. "I love you. Marry me." The young woman burst into tears and the whole restaurant erupted in spontaneous applause. Oysters will always remind me of that moment."

SEA URCHIN TEMPURA

FRESH SEA URCHIN ROE IS WRAPPED IN *SHISO* AND *NORI,* BATTERED AND CRISP-FRIED, TEMPURA-STYLE. SEA URCHIN TEMPURA HAS A DISTINCT SWEETNESS.

INGREDIENTS ——————————————— serves 4

1 sheet dried *nori*, cut into 6 narrow strips of equal size (only 4 strips are used)

8 *shiso* leaves

3 ½ ounces (100g) fresh sea urchin roe

Tempura Batter (page 174)

vegetable oil for deep-frying

sea salt

freshly ground black pepper

2 *sudachi* citrus, halved

METHOD

1. Take one strip of *nori* and put 2 *shiso* leaves at one end. Put a heaping spoonful of sea urchin roe on the *shiso* and roll up in the *nori*. Dab the end of the *nori* with tempura batter to seal. Repeat for the other 3 strips.

2. Bring about 3 inches (8cm) of oil in a deep pot to 340°–350°F (170°–180°C). Dip the rolls whole in tempura batter and deep-fry for up to 3 minutes, until the batter is crisp.

3. Arrange the tempura on a serving dish and serve with sea salt, black pepper and the *sudachi* citrus halves.

BE SURE to use fresh sea urchin which is plump and firm.

"A TIM ZAGAT FAVORITE!

IN FACT, THE RENOWNED RESTAURANT CRITIC never really cared for sea urchin until one day I served him this dish at Matsuhisa. He asked for something different, so on the spur of the moment, with a fresh delivery of sea urchins, I created this tempura. He loved it, and these days eats seven or eight pieces whenever he comes to dinner."

SEA URCHIN

Japanese don't mind the soft, melting orange mound of raw sea urchin roe that so many non-Japanese find unappetizing and insubstantial as a food. With this in mind, I created my Sea Urchin Tempura because I wanted to dispel its ugly image and prove to my customers that sea urchin roe could be delicious. Tempura is an enticing word. When wrapped in *nori* and *shiso* leaves and fried, the sea urchin becomes altogether more appetizing and robust. Cooked sea urchin roe also has a light crunch and sweetness, quite different from the raw variety.

At Matsuhisa in Los Angeles, we keep my treasured ten-year-old sea urchin *shio-kara*, made of sea-urchin scraps pickled in salt and saké and left to ferment. Simply eaten heaped on thinly cut squid sashimi, the salty tang of sea urchin *shio-kara* is the perfect accompaniment to saké—lots of it.

SPINACH-WRAPPED SEA URCHIN WITH EGG SAUCE

THE VIVID GREEN, YELLOW AND ORANGE PALETTE OF SPINACH, EGG SAUCE AND
SALMON ROE HIGHLIGHTS AN INTERESTING MATCH OF THE SWEETNESS OF THE SEA URCHIN
AND THE TANG OF THE SAUCE.

INGREDIENTS ———————————————————————————————— serves 4

28 large spinach leaves

sea salt

5 1/2 ounces (160g) fresh sea urchin roe

4 *shiitake* mushrooms, about 2 inches (5–6 cm) in diameter, stems removed

Egg Sauce (use 4 egg yolks: page 170)

4 tablespoons salmon roe

METHOD

1. Blanch the spinach in a pot of boiling water to which a pinch of sea salt has been added. Plunge the spinach briefly into iced water, remove and pat dry with a paper towel.

2. Pile a generous amount of sea urchin roe on top of each upturned *shiitake* mushroom cap to form a well-rounded mound.

3. Arrange 7 spinach leaves with the stalks at the center and the leaves radiating outward. Place a filled mushroom cap at the center of the leaf pattern and enfold with one spinach leaf at a time. Repeat with the remaining *shiitake* and spinach.

4. Move the wrapped mushrooms to a plate, cover loosely with plastic wrap and microwave for 2 minutes.

5. Spread the Egg Sauce on 4 plates and arrange a mushroom on each. The mushrooms should be cut in half to show the inside. Spoon the salmon roe in between the halves.

MICROWAVING THIS DISH not only cuts down the cooking time but brings out the green color of the spinach nicely.

SHRIMP, LOBSTER AND CRAB

SHRIMP

I adore the larger shrimp varieties, such as the Santa Barbara shrimp caught around Los Angeles (and its Japanese cousin, the *botan* shrimp), Dublin Bay Prawns from Britain and Japanese *kuruma* shrimp. Japan is fortunate in that its seas are home to a rich variety of shrimp and lobster. At the Tsukiji fish market in Tokyo—probably the only market in the world to have so many types of seafood under one roof—shoppers are spoiled by the variety of shrimp.

Shrimp can be fried, steamed, boiled or grilled. To my mind, nothing beats a little light grilling. Traditionally, sushi chefs boil shrimp, a technique that robs it of its natural sweetness. To lock in this sweetness, it is crucial that the shrimp is only partially cooked—say 70% to 80%—as in my Scampi with Spicy Lemon Garlic Sauce (page 50). Because I like the natural and authentic taste of quality ingredients, I believe that fresh food is enjoyed best raw, or at the very least, with only the minimum of cooking.

Spicy Lemon Garlic Sauce will also complement crab and scallop. Shrimp, scallops and crab are all delicious simply grilled, but adding this tangy sauce, or perhaps *ponzu* (page 174), makes for a more exciting dining experience. No doubt, my fervent use of lemon stems from the time I lived in Peru. It is never enough for me just to squeeze some lemon juice over fried or grilled food. I need to uniformly distribute the fruit's citric acidity in a sauce. Spicy Sour Botan Shrimp (page 54) also features a piquant sauce, although the stir-fry cooking method is more Chinese in style. There should be no hard-and-fast rules about cooking. Despite my training as a sushi chef and personal preference for raw shrimp, I wouldn't dream of only serving shrimp as sashimi or sushi. On the contrary, I pride myself on creating dishes that entice and thrill my customers, and this sustains my creative energy.

Popular home-cooked dishes in Japan include deep-fried shrimp and tempura served with either a dipping sauce or salt. I jazzed up tempura for my American customers with Kuruma Shrimp Tempura with Creamy Spicy Sauce (page 52), which mixes the sauce with the tempura instead of serving it on the side. Outside Japan, I sometimes use rock shrimp instead of *kuruma* shrimp.

CRAB

America may not enjoy the same variety of crab as Japan, but the serving methods are inspired: from using a hammer to smash open steamed Dungeness crab on the West Coast to a delicate blue-crab soup on the East Coast.

My customers love crab but complain it is messy and difficult to eat. But even ladies with the loveliest nails need not fear my Snow Crab Roll with Caviar (page 62). Frothing Blue Crab (page 64) is an altogether more complicated dish, at least for the chef: The crab is cooked, flaked, stuffed back in its shell, covered with meringue and fried. All the customers have to do is pick up a pair of chopsticks. And they certainly appreciate that.

MATSUHISA SHRIMP

The NATURAL SWEETNESS of LIGHTLY GRILLED shrimp is complemented by the SALTINESS of caviar, the citrus BOUQUET of *yuzu* with *shiso*, and the SECRET ingredient: Spicy Creamy Sauce.

INGREDIENTS ———————————————————————— serves 4

4 fresh *kuruma* shrimp, about 1 ounce (30g) each

vegetable oil for deep-frying

1 tablespoon clarified butter (page 173)

1 *shiitake* mushroom, stem removed, sliced lengthwise in 4 pieces

2 *shiso* leaves, cut in half lengthwise

a little Creamy Spicy Sauce (page 170)

4 teaspoons osetra caviar

2 teaspoons *yuzu* juice

sudachi citrus, halved, for garnish

METHOD

1. Prepare the shrimp: Remove the heads, then shell and devein. Rinse briefly under cold water and drain. Deep-fry the heads in oil and set aside.

2. Make a slit down the middle of the shrimp as far as the tail and lightly score lines all over the shrimp with the heel of a knife blade. (This *ha-uchi* technique, page 19, prevents the shrimp from curling up when cooked.)

3. Heat the clarified butter in a small frying pan over medium heat and sauté the mushroom until limp.

4. Preheat a grill or broiler. On the slit side of each shrimp, add a piece of mushroom and half a *shiso* leaf with a dab of Creamy Spicy Sauce. Grill or broil for 1 minute until the surface of the shrimp just turns opaque.

5. Transfer the shrimp to a serving dish, top each with a teaspoon of caviar and 1/2 teaspoon of *yuzu* juice. Serve with the deep-fried shrimp heads and garnish with the halved *sudachi* citrus.

I CREATED THIS DISH WITH SHRIMP and scallop when I was asked to make finger food for a cocktail party. Pop the whole morsel in your mouth!

SCAMPI WITH SPICY LEMON GARLIC SAUCE

I LOVE shrimp DRENCHED with an AROMATIC sauce of saké, soy sauce, ginger, garlic and TANGY lemon.

INGREDIENTS ———————————————————————————————— serves 4

4 fresh scampi, about 10 ½ ounces (300g) each

sea salt

freshly ground black pepper

young celery with leaves

1 cup (200ml) Spicy Lemon Garlic Sauce (page 172)

METHOD

1. Preheat the oven to 475°F (250°C, gas 9). Split the scampi in half through the shell and sprinkle the flesh with a little sea salt and black pepper.

2. Preheat a grill or broiler. Grill or broil the scampi, shell side down, over high heat for 2 to 3 minutes, until the flesh turns opaque. Cook 3 to 4 minutes more in the oven.

3. Lay the celery in a serving dish, arrange the scampi to the side and pour plenty of Spicy Lemon Garlic Sauce over all.

SPICY LEMON GARLIC SAUCE is great with lobster too.

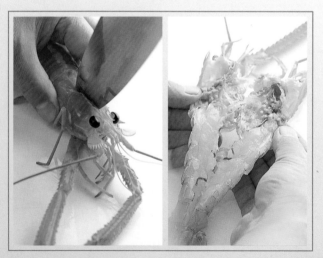

Preparing the scampi

KURUMA SHRIMP TEMPURA WITH CREAMY SPICY SAUCE

POUR CREAMY SPICY SAUCE OVER SHRIMP TEMPURA. CRISP-FRIED SHRIMP LEGS ADD A NEW TEXTURE.

INGREDIENTS ————————————————————————————————— serves 4

12 small *kuruma* shrimp, about ⅔ ounce (20g) each

vegetable oil for deep-frying

1 tablespoon clarified butter (page 173)

4 *shiitake* mushrooms, stems removed

Tempura Batter (page 174)

4 tablespoons Creamy Spicy Sauce (page 170)

1 teaspoon *yuzu* juice

chopped chives

METHOD

1. Prepare the shrimp: Remove the heads, then shell and devein. Rinse briefly in cold water and drain. Remove the legs from the head (discarding head) and reserve for deep-frying in step 3.

2. Heat a medium frying pan on medium heat, add the clarified butter and sauté the mushrooms. Remove to a mixing bowl.

3. Bring about 3 inches (8 cm) of oil in a medium pot to 340°F (170°C). Dip the shrimp in the tempura batter and fry for 1 to 2 minutes. Drain on paper towels. Fry the reserved shrimp legs (without batter). Drain.

4. Add the fried shrimp and Creamy Spicy Sauce to the mushrooms, then add the *yuzu* juice. Add the fried shrimp legs last as they crumble easily.

5. Transfer the shrimp and mushrooms to a serving dish and decorate with chopped chives.

AT THE MATSUHISA SUSHI BAR, customers who order raw sweet shrimp (*ama-ebi*) are delighted when we serve the heads, fried. Some even try to order just the heads—but that is a no-no. After all, each shrimp only has one head.

SPICY SOUR BOTAN SHRIMP

PLUMP AND JUICY SHRIMP ARE SAUTÉED IN BUTTER AND MIXED WITH
A SAUCE COMBINING SOY SAUCE, CHILI GARLIC SAUCE AND LEMON JUICE.

INGREDIENTS ————————————————————————————— serves 4

8 fresh *botan* shrimp, about 1 ½ ounces (40g) each

sea salt

freshly ground black pepper

1 broccoli floret, cut at stems

2 tablespoons clarified butter (page 173)

8 tablespoons Spicy Sour Sauce (page 172)

3 ½ ounces (100g) *enoki* mushrooms

10 chives, cut into lengths about 1 ½ inches (4 cm)

METHOD

1. Prepare the shrimp: Remove the heads, then shell and devein. Rinse briefly in cold water and drain. Sprinkle with a little sea salt and black pepper.

2. Bring a small pot of water to a boil and add a pinch of sea salt. Add the broccoli and boil for 1 ½ minutes. Plunge briefly into iced water and drain.

3. Heat a medium frying pan over high heat. Add the butter and sauté the shrimp. When the shrimp turn opaque, add the Spicy Sour Sauce, broccoli, mushrooms and chives and stir-fry briefly.

4. Transfer to a serving dish.

BOTAN SHRIMP HAVE SUCCULENT, sweet flesh. Scallops are also delectable sautéed and served with Spicy Sour Sauce.

KURUMA SHRIMP FILO WITH CILANTRO SAUCE

THE SWEETNESS OF DEEP-FRIED *KURUMA* SHRIMP WRAPPED IN THE DELICATE CRUNCH OF FILO IS OFFSET BY A STRIKING GREEN SAUCE MADE OF CILANTRO.

INGREDIENTS ——————————————————————— serves 4

Sauce

½ ounce (15g) cilantro (coriander) leaves

2 teaspoons extra virgin olive oil

1 tablespoon plus 2 teaspoons rice vinegar

sea salt to taste

4 fresh *kuruma* shrimp, about 1 ounce (30g) each

Tempura Batter (page 174)

3 ½ ounces (100g) shredded filo

vegetable oil for deep-frying

METHOD

1. Make the sauce: Grind the cilantro leaves to a paste in a ceramic mortar and then mix in the remaining sauce ingredients. Set aside.

2. Prepare the shrimp: Remove the heads, then shell and devein. Rinse briefly in cold water and drain. Remove the legs from the head (discarding head) and reserve for deep-frying in step 4.

3. Insert a wooden skewer into the shrimp from the tail end. Dip the shrimp in tempura batter and then, starting from the tail, wrap the filo around the shrimp until the shrimp is hidden. Filo dries out easily, so sandwich each wrapped shrimp between sheets of dampened paper towels.

4. Bring 3 inches (8 cm) of oil in a small, deep saucepan to 340°F (170°C). Fry the shrimp until the filo is crisp. Swirl the shrimp around when frying to ensure the filo doesn't unravel. Remove the wooden skewers. Fry the reserved shrimp legs (without batter). Drain.

5. Arrange the shrimp with the fried legs on a serving dish and spoon the sauce around them.

FILO IS AVAILABLE ALREADY SHREDDED and frozen from stores that sell Greek and Near-Eastern ingredients.

"I FIRST CAME ACROSS CILANTRO

WHEN I LIVED IN PERU. There is a Peruvian chicken and rice dish called *arroz con pollo* containing cooked cilantro. When I was served this at a friend's house, I found the unfamiliar smell of the cooked cilantro completely unappetizing. But when I found out that cilantro was widely eaten throughout Asia and Latin America, I regretted not having the stomach for it. So I experimented with ways to eat it; incorporating it in fried dishes, in Japanese clear soup with jalapeño and lemon, in sashimi even. Before I knew it, cilantro had turned into something I missed when it wasn't in the food. Now, I find it indispensable: Ceviche, in particular, tastes bland without it."

SPINY LOBSTER SOUP

THIS SIMPLE SOUP OF *DASHI* AND LOBSTER IS GIVEN A NOVEL TWIST WITH
THE ADDITION OF JALAPEÑO AND *YUZU*.

INGREDIENTS ———————————————— serves 4

½ white scallion (spring onion)

2 live spiny lobsters, about 14 ounces (400g) each

sea salt

Soup

2 ¼ cups (440ml) Dashi (page 174)

2 teaspoons light soy sauce

2 teaspoons saké

¼ teaspoon sea salt

a little juice, squeezed from finely grated ginger (page 20)

menegi for garnish

yuzu citrus rind, sliced into thin strips

1 jalapeño, sliced into fine rounds

"IN MEXICO,
I WAS IMPRESSED BY
HOW THE FLAVOR OF STEWS
and seafood soups was radically
changed by the addition of
jalapeño, cilantro and lemon
as condiments. Japanese cooks
wouldn't dream of adding jalapeño
to a traditional lobster soup made
with *dashi*, but I enjoy the free-
dom of juggling contrasting flavors, and I like spicy tastes. So I
dropped in a bit of jalapeño
and this is the result."

METHOD

1. Finely shred the scallion until it resembles coarse strands of white hair
(the *shiraga negi* cutting technique). Soak under barely running cold water
for 5 minutes to remove any astringency and then drain.

2. Insert a knife between the lobster head and body and pull apart. With
the knife, split the heads and bodies in half vertically.

3. Add a pinch of sea salt to a large pot of boiling water. Add the lobster,
keeping the heat on high. Remove the lobster pieces when the shells have
turned vivid red.

4. Make the soup: Bring the *dashi* to a near-boil in a large saucepan over high
heat. Add the light soy sauce and saké. Adjust the flavor with sea salt. Add the
lobster and bring to a boil again briefly. Turn off the heat and add the juice from
the grated ginger.

5. Remove the lobster pieces and divide among 4 soup dishes. Top with the scallion
shreds, *menegi* and strips of *yuzu* rind. Pour the soup around the lobster and scatter with
the jalapeño rounds.

LOBSTER IS PREBOILED to prevent it from clouding the soup.

SPICY SEA-URCHIN-GRILLED KING CRAB

LEGS OF KING CRAB ARE SPREAD WITH A GENEROUS DOLLOP OF SEA URCHIN ROE AND GRILLED IN THIS DYNAMIC DISH. IF CRABMEAT PLUMPS AND SWELLS OVER ITS SHELL WHEN COOKED, IT'S A SIGN OF FRESHNESS.

INGREDIENTS — serves 4

Sauce

3 ½ ounces (100g) fresh sea urchin roe

2 teaspoons Chinese chili bean sauce

1 teaspoon light soy sauce

1 teaspoon saké

4 fresh king crab legs, about 5–7 ounces (150–200g) for each leg

3 ½ ounces (100g) leeks, white part only

vegetable oil for deep-frying

2 lemons, halved

METHOD

1. Make the sauce: Mix the sauce ingredients together in a small bowl and set aside.

2. Preheat a grill or broiler. Lay the crab legs flat. Trim off the shell along the top of the crab legs with a knife. Grill the legs, shell side down, over high heat on a wire rack until about 50% to 60% cooked through, or until the shell has turned red. Remove from the grill.

3. Preheat a grill or broiler. Brush the crabmeat with the sauce and grill or broil until the surface browns. Brush with more sauce 2 or 3 times during the cooking process. Set aside.

4. Cut the leeks into 3-inch (8-cm) pieces. Make a vertical slit down the middle of each piece as far as the center and pry open. Slice lengthwise into thin julienne strips. Bring about 3 inches (8 cm) of oil in a deep saucepan to 320°F (160°C). Fry the leek shreds until crisp. Drain on paper towels.

5. Arrange the crab legs on a serving plate and garnish with the lemon halves and fried leek shreds.

SNOW CRAB ROLL WITH CAVIAR

CRABMEAT IS ROLLED IN PÂTE BRIQUE FOR EASY EATING IN THIS SIMPLE COMBINATION OF
SWEET CRAB WITH SALTY CAVIAR.

INGREDIENTS ———————————————————————————————— serves 4

1 live snow crab, about 1 1/2–1 3/4 pounds (600–700g)

2 sheets pâte brique

menegi to taste

2 1/2 tablespoons osetra caviar

4 large lettuce (or salad) leaves

chervil sprigs for garnish

METHOD

1. Steam the crab whole for 20 minutes over high heat. Remove the meat from the shell, reserving several claws for decoration.

2. Preheat a grill or broiler. Cut each sheet of pâte brique in half to make 4 semicircles. Place the crabmeat in the middle and the *menegi* and caviar on top of the crab. Fold each side of the pâte-brique semicircles over the fillings one side at a time and then roll up away from you. Grill or broil until crisp and slightly brown.

3. Lay the lettuce leaves on the bottom of a serving dish, add the crab rolls and garnish with the reserved crab claws and chervil sprigs.

4. The rolls are eaten wrapped in the leaves.

PÂTE BRIQUE IS A NORTH AFRICAN PASTRY made from water, flour, salt and vegetable oil. The dough is boiled, making the surface rough like a brick. The pastry is sold in circular sheets.

FROTHING BLUE CRAB

Steamed blue crab meat is STUFFED into the shell and covered with SEA URCHIN ROE and stiffly beaten egg whites. The cooked egg-white mixture resembles the BUBBLES that FROTH from a live crab.

INGREDIENTS ———————————————————————— serves 4

4 fresh blue crabs, about 7 ounces
   (200g) each

4 egg whites

4 tablespoons flying fish roe

3 1/2 ounces (100g) fresh sea urchin roe

vegetable oil for deep-frying

fresh *wakame*

1 stalk *hajikami* (page 174) per serving

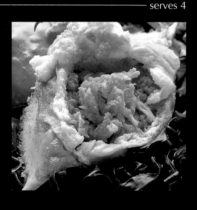

METHOD

1. Steam the crabs whole over high heat for 20 minutes.

2. Beat the egg whites until standing in stiff peaks.

3. Separate the crab body from the shell and remove the meat, yellow mustard and roe
   (if any). Mix everything together in a medium bowl.

4. Stuff the shells with the crabmeat mixture and flying fish roe, cover with the sea urchin roe
   and then smooth the beaten egg over the top.

5. Bring about 3 inches (8cm) of oil in a large saucepan to 340°F (170°C). Slip the crabs, shell side down,
   into the hot oil and deep-fry until the beaten egg puffs up. Do not turn over.

6. Spread the *wakame* out on a serving dish, arrange the crabs on top and serve with a stalk of *hajikami*.

THIS DISH IS BEST SERVED when just fried and piping hot.

OCTOPUS AND SQUID

Along with white fish and shellfish, octopus is one of my favorite seafoods. Like most Japanese, I don't find the soft, squirmy appearance of a live octopus—sometimes called "devilfish"—as unappetizing as others. Moreover, I relish the juicy chewiness of it that many find unpleasant.

To many Westerners, if they have eaten octopus at all, the most familiar preparation may be the tender, stewed chunks of octopus found in Italian restaurants rather than the textured bite and suckers-and-all of Japanese-style octopus. Hence people are immediately put off when they try octopus in sushi restaurants. This is why I recommend traditional Japanese tenderizing methods, such as beating the octopus with a *daikon* before boiling, and the *ha-uchi* technique (page 19), which involves making fine incisions across its flesh with the heel of a knife (this reduces chewiness and increases its ability to absorb sauces). *Ha-uchi* is also recommended for shellfish and squid. I also avoid serving sushi and sashimi to people who claim not to like octopus, in favor of more enticing preparations that may change the image they have of octopus.

I often suggest trying my Spicy Octopus Salad (page 70) to diners reluctant to eat octopus. My tiradito (page 74) or New Style Sashimi (page 116) have also helped my customers lose their old resistance to this delicious mollusc. Indeed, one regular Nobu New York customer always orders octopus sashimi and sushi for takeout as well.

Japan has dozens of varieties of octopus. The recipes introduced here use three kinds: the commonest (*madako*); the largest, known as the North Pacific giant octopus; and the small baby octopus. As octopus spoils quickly, I cook them live, just enough to retain their unique chewy texture. I urge you to look for a *madako* octopus and boil or grill it according to my instructions on the following pages. Try eating it with just lemon juice and sea salt and I'm sure you will soon appreciate the taste and texture. It would be wonderful, too, if everyone could experience the very different taste of raw octopus.

PREPARING OCTOPUS

1. Removing the sliminess

Use a knife to cut a slit around the beak of a live common octopus. (The beak can be found where the tentacles join the head.) Remove the beak with your fingers. Next, turn the head inside out, and pull out the ink sac, the innards and the eggs, if any. Then rinse the head well under cold running water. Remove excess sinews with your fingers or a knife.

Turn the head back out the right way and place it in a ceramic mortar (a regular bowl won't work) without removing the skin. Put your hand inside the head and rub the octopus around the mortar. The sliminess appears as small white bubbles a bit like beaten egg white. Continue rubbing the octopus around the mortar for five to ten minutes, until all the sliminess and any sand clinging to the suckers have been removed. If you add salt at this stage, the slime can be removed more quickly, but I don't do this as salt will also toughen the flesh.

When all the sliminess has gone, rinse well. Turn out the head again and rinse all folds and creases thoroughly, as well as the tips of the tentacles. If the octopus still feels slimy, rub it around the mortar once more. Be sure to rinse well. If you skip the slime-removing stage, the octopus will end up smelling fishy when cooked.

2. Tenderizing

The common octopus can be further tenderized by pounding the tentacles with a *daikon* before boiling. Use a cut raw radish about the size of a rolling pin. You should pound the tentacles with just enough force not to snap the *daikon*. Pounding softens its fibers and makes the octopus tender when it is boiled. If the inside of the tentacles still feels hard to the touch, keep pounding until it feels softer.

3. Boiling

Bring to a boil enough water to cover the octopus and add salt. The salt-to-water ratio should be 3% salt to water, or 1 ounce (30g) salt to 1 quart (1l) of water. Slowly slip the octopus into the water, tentacles first. This is partly so that the legs curl and bunch up, making an attractive shape, and also to avoid a sudden drop in water temperature, which would occur if you put the whole octopus in at once.

Keep the heat on high until the water comes back to a boil, then partially cover and simmer on medium heat for 30 to 45 minutes. The heat should be between low and medium, just high enough so that the octopus is not jiggling about. If this happens, the skin will come off. Be careful not to stir it around with chopsticks, as this too will abrade the skin. The cooking time varies slightly according to the size of the octopus.

Usually the octopus is removed from the water after boiling, but I turn off the heat and leave it in the pot of water to cool. This makes the octopus even more tender.

4. Using every last scrap

Meat scraps from the head and tentacles can be cut into bite-size pieces and used to make ceviche (page 118). It would be fun to gather together some adventurous friends for an octopus feast. I want everyone to try this wonderful yet still unfamiliar food.

SPICY OCTOPUS SALAD

Served as a SALAD, octopus is complemented by the ZEST of *YUZU* citrus and the PUNGENCY of chili bean sauce.

INGREDIENTS ————————————————————————— serves 4

Sauce

1 clove ginger, finely grated

2 teaspoons Chinese chili bean sauce

2 teaspoons soy sauce

4 teaspoons *yuzu* juice

sesame oil

2 tablespoons extra virgin olive oil

sea salt

freshly ground black pepper

2 tentacles *madako* octopus, 7 ounces (200g) each, boiled (page 69)

20 chives, cut into 1-inch (3-cm) pieces

4 ounces (100g) *enoki* mushrooms, cut into 1-inch (3-cm) pieces

3 ½ ounces (100g) salad greens (celery stalk, mâche, onion sprouts and mustard greens used here)

METHOD

1. Make the sauce: Mix the ginger in a bowl with the chili bean sauce, soy sauce and *yuzu* juice. Add a few drops of sesame oil and all of the extra virgin olive oil and mix again. Add sea salt and black pepper to taste. Set aside.

2. Cut the tentacles into bite-size pieces and combine with the chives and *enoki* mushrooms in a bowl. Add the sauce and toss gently. Serve with the salad greens.

AS AN ALTERNATIVE TO OCTOPUS, briefly boiled squid also works nicely.

BABY OCTOPUS WITH TRUFFLES AND YUZU JUICE

FOR THIS DISH, BABY OCTOPUS IS BOILED BRIEFLY AND SERVED WARM. THE OCTOPUS HAS A NICE SOFT YET CHEWY TEXTURE. WITH A TOP NOTE OF TRUFFLES, THE DISH IS FURTHER ACCENTED BY SEA SALT AND THE ACIDITY OF YUZU.

INGREDIENTS ———————————————————————————————————— serves 4

4 fresh baby octopuses

sea salt

1 tablespoon *yuzu* juice

8 thin slices truffle

truffle oil

sansho sprig for garnish, optional (see page 91)

METHOD

1. Cut out and remove the beak from each octopus. Push out the eyes from behind and cut them off with a knife. Turn the head inside out and remove the ink sac and innards. If the head cavity contains eggs, remove them as well. Wash the inside of the head cavity thoroughly.

2. Put plenty of sea salt in a ceramic mortar (or bowl) and remove the slime from each octopus (page 68). Rinse. Cut the head from the tentacles but keep the tentacles in one piece.

3. Bring to a boil enough water to cover the octopus in a medium pot and add a pinch of sea salt. Put the octopus in the pot and boil over high heat for about **20** seconds.

4. Drain the octopus pieces in a colander, then arrange them on a serving plate while still hot.

5. Sprinkle sea salt over the octopus and drizzle with the *yuzu* juice. Top with the truffle slices, add 2 or 3 drops of truffle oil and decorate with a *sansho* sprig.

I HAVE A FAVORITE RESTAURANT (OSTERIA DA FIORE) in Venice, where I encountered the baby octopus dish that inspired my own. It was a simple preparation of fresh baby octopus sautéed briefly in olive oil and seasoned with sea salt.

OCTOPUS TIRADITO, NOBU STYLE

ENJOY THE TEXTURE AND FLAVOR OF RAW OCTOPUS, ENHANCED BY CILANTRO AND CHILI PASTE.

INGREDIENTS ———————————————————————————————————— serves 4

1 tentacle North Pacific giant octopus, 2 ¼ pounds (1 kg)

sea salt

cilantro (coriander) leaves

rocoto chili paste

1 tablespoon plus 1 teaspoon *yuzu* juice

2 tablespoons plus 2 teaspoons lemon juice

thin cucumber slices

benibana (safflower) for garnish, optional

METHOD

1. Starting at the thickest end, cut along the row of suckers on the tentacle. Gradually remove the skin as you work the knife sideways underneath the suckers.

2. Place the skin with suckers attached in a ceramic mortar or bowl and knead with plenty of salt to remove the slime and grit inside the suckers. Rinse. Bring a small pot of water to a boil and add a pinch of sea salt. Add the octopus skin and boil for about 5 minutes. Remove octopus skin and drain. Cut out the suckers to use later for decoration.

3. Use a kitchen cloth to gently rub off the membrane covering the skinned tentacle. Rinse the tentacle briefly in cold salted water and wipe dry with paper towels.

4. Slice the tentacle as thinly as possible, between about ¹⁄₁₆ and ⅛ inch (2–4mm) thick.

5. Arrange the octopus slices attractively on a plate. Place a cilantro leaf in the middle of each slice. Add a sucker to each and top with a small dollop of chili paste. Drizzle with the *yuzu* and lemon juice. Decorate with thinly sliced cucumber.

6. Sprinkle with sea salt to taste. Remember that salt provides the main flavoring here, so the dish will taste bland if you use too little. Decorate with the *benibana* flower.

AFTER WE CLOSE UP AT NIGHT AND RELAX with a drink, this is the snack I like to order. I love Octopus Tiradito, White Fish Tiradito, Scallop Tiradito, Oyster Tiradito—come to think of it, any sort of tiradito.

OCTOPUS SHABU-SHABU WITH SPICY UME SAUCE

UMEBOSHI IS A TYPICAL AND TRADITIONAL JAPANESE PRESERVE WITH A UNIQUE TART FLAVOR AND PURPORTED HEALTH BENEFITS.

INGREDIENTS ———————————————————————————————— serves 4

Sauce

2 tablespoons *umeboshi* pulp, passed through a sieve, or commercial *umeboshi* paste

½ teaspoon light soy sauce

rocoto chili paste

¼ cup (50ml) Dashi (page 174)

sea salt

1 tentacle North Pacific giant octopus, 2 ¼ pounds (1 kg)

shiso buds for garnish, optional

METHOD

1. Make the sauce: Put the *umeboshi* pulp or paste in a bowl with the soy sauce and rocoto chili paste. Add the *dashi* a little at a time to thin the mixture. The finished sauce should be slightly thick. Adjust the flavor with sea salt, if necessary. Chill and set aside.

2. Starting at the thickest end, cut along the row of suckers on the tentacle. Gradually remove the skin as you work the knife sideways underneath the suckers.

3. Use a kitchen cloth to gently rub off the membrane covering the skinned tentacle. Rinse the tentacle briefly in cold salted water and wipe dry with paper towels.

4. Slice the tentacle as thinly as possible, between about ¹⁄₁₆ and ⅛ inch (3–4mm) thick.

5. Bring a small pot of water to a boil, add a pinch of sea salt and immerse a few octopus slices at a time for 2 to 3 seconds. Plunge the slices into a bowl of iced water and drain in a colander.

6. Place the octopus slices on a serving dish over crushed ice and decorate with the *shiso* buds. Serve the sauce separately.

SALT IS ADDED TO BRING OUT THE FLAVOR OF OCTOPUS when it is boiled briefly, but be careful not to oversalt. Other light, refreshing sauces that go well with Octopus Shabu-shabu are *ponzu* (page 174), Yuzu Dressing (page 173) and Matsuhisa Dressing (page 171).

"FOR ME, THE TASTE OF *UMEBOSHI* PLUMS WITH WHITE RICE, PICKLES AND *MISO* SOUP is a very nostalgic one. When you don't have an appetite or feel under the weather, place an *umeboshi* in a tea cup; add dried bonito flakes, finely grated ginger, chopped white scallions (spring onions) and a little soy sauce; pour hot water over it and drink.

There are many grades of *umeboshi*. A high-grade *umeboshi* is more than just tart, it has an intense, complex flavor which produces a wonderful sauce. I know that for many people this mouth-puckering flavor is an acquired taste, but for the few who do acquire it, it becomes a favorite."

GRILLED OCTOPUS WITH MISO ANTICUCHO SAUCE

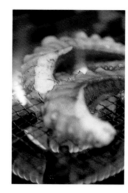

FRESH OCTOPUS IS LIGHTLY GRILLED TO BRING OUT ITS SWEETNESS, AND SERVED WITH A COMBINATION OF PERUVIAN *ANTICUCHO* SAUCE AND JAPANESE *MISO*.

INGREDIENTS ———————————————————————————————————— serves 4

Red Sauce

½ cup (115g) red *miso*

½ cup (100ml) Aji Panca Sauce (page 170)

Yellow Sauce

½ cup (130g) Nobu-style Saikyo Miso, (page 172)

½ cup (100ml) Aji Amarillo Sauce (page 170)

sea salt

freshly ground black pepper

2 tentacles fresh *madako* octopus, 7 ounces (200g) each, cleaned and prepared (page 68)

giboshi leaves for garnish, optional

METHOD

1. Make the two sauces by adding the red *miso* to Aji Panca Sauce for the red sauce and Nobu-style Saikyo Miso to Aji Amarillo Sauce for the yellow sauce. The flavor of *miso* differs by maker, so add a little at a time to taste. The finished sauces should be slightly thick.

2. Preheat a grill or broiler. Sprinkle sea salt and black pepper on the octopus and grill on a wire rack. Turn the tentacles during grilling, and be careful not to overcook: The octopus should be 70% cooked. In general, it should be taken off the grill when the tips of the tentacles have curled up as far as they can. Slice the tentacles into bite-size pieces and set aside.

3. Put the two sauces side by side on a plate with the octopus on top. Decorate with *giboshi* leaves.

AT MATSUHISA ASPEN WE SERVE THIS SAUCE with Colorado lamb, a favorite of mine.

"WHEN I WAS IN PERU, I USED TO ENJOY DRINKING BEER EATING *ANTICUCHO*, a popular snack served at soccer-ground concessions. *Anticucho* is charcoal-grilled beef heart on a skewer, reminiscent of Japan's grilled chicken *yakitori*. After being marinated in a red sauce and basting with oil during grilling, the meat is slathered with a yellow sauce and eaten with a salsa of choice. I also used to drink *chicha*, the common alcoholic drink in Peru. It is traditionally made by women chewing raw corn, then spitting out the mixture into an earthenware jar where it is left to ferment. I was rather taken aback when I heard this.

I added *anticucho* to my menu after discovering a Latin American working at Matsuhisa in Los Angeles who knew about *anticucho*. Together we bought the spices and tried different combinations, with me calling Peru for advice, and this is the sauce I came up with. Instead of beef heart, I use Kobe beef, chicken and salmon, as well as scallops and vegetables."

SQUID

My customers were as leery of squid as they were of octopus. My sushi did nothing to change their image of squid as being tough and chewy, so I created Squid Pasta with Light Garlic Sauce (page 82), a stir-fry of squid with asparagus and *shiitake* mushrooms. Customers were initially attracted by the word "pasta," and when they found that stir-fried squid is crunchy rather than chewy, many became hooked and went on to enjoy squid sushi and sashimi as well.

My Baby Squid Tempura with Squid Ink Sauce (page 84) is a more refined version of the popular calamari: The batter is light and crisp while the squid inside is barely cooked to retain its fresh flavor.

Squid can generally be divided into two types: cuttlefish, which has a cuttlebone in its body, and squid, which doesn't. The tender flesh of cuttlefish is ideal for sautéing and tempura. Japanese tempura restaurants generally serve sweet, smaller varieties like *mongo* cuttlefish and *aori* squid. Black Rice-Stuffed Squid (page 86) uses *yariika*, a long, spearlike squid with thin flesh good for stuffing and also for sashimi, a favorite of mine.

The Japanese also eat squid as *ika somen*, very thin slivers of squid masquerading as *somen* noodles (page 25), which is eaten with a dipping sauce (page 24) or soy sauce with finely grated ginger. If you want to try making *ika somen*, just remember to cut down the length of the squid along the grain; otherwise it will be chewy. And remember to slurp when you eat!

PREPARING SQUID

1. Lay the squid on a chopping board and, holding the head with one hand, grasp the tentacles at their base and gently pull with the other hand. Remove the quill and throw away the guts, retaining the ink sac if needed. The ink sac is small and silvery dark and usually clearly visible. Cut it carefully out of the innards, trying not to pierce it.

2. Wash the body and remove the thin membrane by hand. Also remove the "wings," which can be clearly seen attached to the body, and retain.

3. Cut away the tentacles just in front of the eyes and squeeze out the small beak. Discard. Rinse and dry with paper towels.

For cuttlefish, cut the head on the cuttle side, open and remove the guts. The ink sac will be attached to the other side. Wash the body well and retain the ink sac, if needed.

AORI SQUID WITH MAUI ONION SALSA

AORI SQUID DOESN'T TOUGHEN WHEN COOKED. HERE IT IS SPRINKLED WITH SALT AND PEPPER, AND LIGHTLY GRILLED TO BRING OUT ITS SWEETNESS.

INGREDIENTS ———————— serves 4

1 fresh *aori* squid, cleaned and prepared (page 80)

sea salt

freshly ground black pepper

4 tablespoons Maui Onion Salsa (page 171)

shiso buds for garnish, optional

tardivo radicchio for garnish, optional

METHOD

1. Pat the squid dry with paper towels. Make a pine-cone pattern of incisions on its surface by cutting with the knife blade at an angle across the flesh one way and then repeating the other way to form a cross-hatching of diagonal incisions.

2. Preheat a grill or broiler to high. Sprinkle a little sea salt and black pepper over the squid. Grill the squid on a wire rack until the surface turns opaque. Cut the squid into 1/2- to 3/4-inch- (1.5–2-cm-) wide pieces.

3. Divide the squid pieces among 4 plates, top with Maui Onion Salsa and garnish with *shiso* buds and radicchio.

SQUID PASTA WITH LIGHT GARLIC SAUCE

MONGO CUTTLEFISH IS CUT TO RESEMBLE CONCHIGLIE PASTA AND SAUTÉED FOR AN EASY-TO-EAT MOUTHFUL. THE SOY SAUCE AND BUTTER FLAVORS OF THIS DISH ARE SHOT THROUGH WITH THE SPICINESS OF *SHICHIMI TOGARASHI.*

INGREDIENTS ——————————————————————————— serves 4

4 broccoli florets, cut into bite-size pieces

sea salt

4 ¼ ounces (120g) fresh *mongo* cuttlefish, cleaned and prepared (page 80)

freshly ground black pepper

4 teaspoons clarified butter (page 173)

1 clove garlic, thinly sliced

4 *shiitake* mushrooms, stems removed

6 spears green asparagus, cut into 2-inch (5-cm) lengths

4 tablespoons Saké Soy Sauce (page 172)

shichimi togarashi to taste

METHOD

1. Boil the broccoli for 1 ½ minutes in a small pot of boiling water to which a pinch of sea salt has been added. Plunge briefly into iced water and drain.

2. Pat the cuttlefish dry with paper towels. Cut the body horizontally into 2-inch- (5-cm-) wide strips. Use a knife to make fine vertical incisions down the length of each strip along the grain. These should be fairly deep, but very close together. (When the cuttlefish cooks and curls, the incisions will give it a conchiglie-like texture.) Cut the cuttlefish parallel to the incisions into ½-inch- (1.5-cm-) wide strips. Sprinkle the strips with a little sea salt and black pepper.

3. Heat a medium frying pan over medium heat. Add the clarified butter and sauté the garlic slices. When the aroma of the garlic has been released, turn the heat up to high, add the *shiitake* mushrooms and fry lightly. Add the cuttlefish, green asparagus and broccoli, in that order, and season with a little sea salt and black pepper.

4. When the cuttlefish is about 70% cooked (the surface turns opaque), add the Saké Soy Sauce in a swirling motion just before turning off the heat. Mix the contents of the pan to distribute the sauce evenly. Place in a serving dish. Add *shichimi togarashi* to taste.

RECOMMENDED FOR THOSE WHO MAY BE a little squeamish or leery of squid and cuttlefish.

BABY SQUID TEMPURA WITH SQUID INK SAUCE

FRESH CALAMARI IS DIPPED IN TEMPURA BATTER AND BRIEFLY DEEP-FRIED. POTATO FLOUR ADDS EXTRA CRUNCH. SAVOR THE COMBINATION OF TEMPURA AND THE SWEETNESS OF SQUID INK.

INGREDIENTS ———————————————————————————————————— serves 4

12 fresh baby squid, ½ ounce (15g) each, cleaned and prepared (see page 80)

vegetable oil for deep-frying

3 tablespoons potato flour

Sauce

Tempura Batter (page 174)

8 tablespoons Dashi (page 174)

cucumber flowers for garnish, optional

2 tablespoons *mirin*

2 tablespoons light soy sauce

2 teaspoons squid ink

1 tablespoon powdered arrowroot starch, dissolved in 4 teaspoons water

METHOD

1. Pat the squid dry with paper towels. If the squid are on the large side, separate the head and the tentacles with a knife. If not, leave whole.

2. Prepare the sauce: In a small saucepan over high heat, bring the *dashi* and the *mirin* to a boil. Add the soy sauce and squid ink. Turn down to medium heat and gradually swirl in the arrowroot solution. Turn off the heat when the sauce has thickened.

3. Bring about 3 inches (8cm) of oil in a medium saucepan to 340°F (170°C). Prepare the batter by adding the potato flour to the tempura batter. Shake a little more potato flour over the surface of each squid, then dip them in the batter. Deep-fry the squid for 2 minutes, gently shaking each squid when it enters the oil so that the tentacles don't bunch up. Dip the cucumber flowers in the batter and fry likewise.

4. Spread the sauce thinly over the bottom of 4 plates and arrange squid and cucumber flowers on top.

MAKE SURE YOU REALLY SLATHER THE TEMPURA PIECES with the sauce.

BLACK RICE-STUFFED SQUID

BLACK RICE, A GLUTINOUS AND ANCIENT VARIETY OF JAPANESE RICE, IS COOKED WITH
YARIIKA TENTACLES AND VEGETABLES AS A STUFFING FOR BRIEFLY BOILED SQUID.

INGREDIENTS
serves 4

1 cup (160g) black rice

1 cup (160g) short-grain white rice

Boiling liquid for rice

3 cups (600ml) Dashi (page 174)

1 ½ tablespoons saké

1 tablespoon *mirin*

1 ½ tablespoons light soy sauce

1 teaspoon sea salt

• • •

¼ burdock root, peeled

¼ carrot, peeled

2 *shiitake* mushrooms, stemmed

2 *yariika* squid, 9–11 ounces (250–300g) each, cleaned and prepared (page 80)

sansho sprigs and 1 stalk *hajikami* (page 174) per serving for garnish, optional

METHOD

1. Rinse the black rice until the water runs clear and soak for 6 hours. Drain. Rinse the white rice until the water runs clear and soak for 30 minutes. Drain.

2. Make the boiling liquid for the rice: Heat the *dashi* in a small saucepan over high heat and add the saké and *mirin*. As soon as the mixture comes to a boil, turn the heat down to low and add the light soy sauce and sea salt. Remove from heat and let cool to room temperature.

3. Pare the burdock root and carrot into thin shavings by making chipping motions with a knife as you rotate the pieces, rather like hand-sharpening a pencil. Soak the burdock root shavings for 20 minutes in a bowl under a slow stream of barely running cold water to remove any astringency. Thinly slice the *shiitake* mushrooms. Set aside.

4. Clean and rinse the mantle of the squid. Also rinse the tentacles. Add a pinch of sea salt to a pot of boiling water. Immerse the squid's mantle only (not the tentacles) for 30 seconds and then drain. Finely chop the tentacles. Set aside.

5. Cook the rice: Use a heavy medium-size saucepan with a heavy lid (if the lid is light, weigh down with a rock or other weight). In the saucepan, place the black and white rice, vegetables and chopped tentacles. Add the cooled boiling liquid and cover. Put the saucepan over high heat, bring to a boil and boil for 1 minute. Turn the heat down to low and cook for 5 minutes. Finally, turn the heat up to high for 10 seconds. Remove from the heat and let the rice sit for 15 minutes. Do not lift the lid until the rice has finished cooking.

6. Stuff the body cavity of the cooked squid with the cooked rice mixture, firmly pressing it down to the very end of the cavity. Cut the stuffed squid into no more than ¾-inch- (2-cm-) wide rings. Arrange on a serving plate and garnish with *sansho* sprigs and *hajikami*.

THIS RECIPE IS SIMPLE TO MAKE IF YOU HAVE an automatic rice cooker at home. The tentacles can be cooked with the rice or done separately. Best served hot, this dish can also be eaten cold.

SQUID INK SOBA

THIS IS THE JAPANESE VERSION OF ITALY'S SQUID INK PASTA.

INGREDIENTS ———————————————————— serves 4

Soba dipping sauce

1 ½ cups (300ml) Dashi (page 174)

2 tablespoons *mirin*

4 tablespoons soy sauce

2 tablespoons plus 1 teaspoon granulated sugar

1 ounce (30g) dried bonito flakes

3 cups (360g) buckwheat (*soba*) flour

1 ½ cups (150g) all-purpose (plain) flour

1 tablespoon squid ink

1 cup (200ml) water

METHOD

1. Make the *soba* dipping sauce: Heat the *dashi* in a small saucepan over high heat, add the *mirin*, soy sauce and granulated sugar. Add the bonito flakes just before the sauce comes to a boil and turn off the heat. After the bonito flakes have sunk to the bottom, strain the sauce and cool.

2. Mix the buckwheat and all-purpose flours in a large bowl thoroughly with your hands. Mix the squid ink and water in a separate bowl. Pour half of the squid ink and water mixture into the flour mixture. Mix together steadily with your hands.

3. When the texture of the *soba* dough resembles coarse breadcrumbs, add the remaining squid ink and water mixture and knead the dough until it comes together into a ball and has a consistency and density similar to an earlobe.

4. Sprinkle buckwheat flour over the dough as you roll it out with a rolling pin to a thickness of ¹⁄₁₆ inch (1 mm). Fold the dough into a neat 8-inch- (20-cm-) wide strip. Cut the dough across the folds into ¹⁄₁₆-inch- (1-mm-) wide noodles.

5. Bring a large pot of water to a boil. Add the *soba* and boil for 1 minute. Drain lightly.

6. Arrange the *soba* noodles on a bamboo sieve and serve with the dipping sauce.

ACCORDING TO THE SEASON, I sometimes knead shredded *shiso* leaves or green tea into the *soba* dough.

"NOODLE VARIETIES ARE BOTH POPULAR AND PLENTIFUL IN JAPAN, WHETHER SERVED IN HOT SOUP or dipped in cold sauce, and eaten both at home and in noodle restaurants. At home most Japanese boil dried *soba* or *udon*, but some make them fresh. All my restaurants serve nutritious, low-calorie *soba*. My regular menu includes Soba Risotto (page 154), which is a Japanese-style risotto using buckwheat groats in place of rice."

FAIRY SQUID WITH KINOME SU-MISO SAUCE

As they flood the PALATE, the TASTE of fairy squid and the FRAGRANCE of *sansho* sprigs (*KINOME*) always suggest early SUMMER in Japan.

INGREDIENTS ——————————————————————— serves 4

Sauce

1 ounce (30g) *sansho* sprigs

3/4 cup (200g) Nobu-style Saikyo Miso (page 172)

1/4 cup (50ml) rice vinegar

1 teaspoon light soy sauce

sea salt

16 boiled fairy squid, 3 1/2 ounces (100g) in total

strips of *yuzu* citrus and lime rind for garnish, optional

METHOD

1. Make the sauce: Grind the *sansho* sprigs to a paste in a ceramic mortar. Add in order the Nobu-style Saikyo Miso, rice vinegar and soy sauce and grind together. Add a little sea salt to adjust the flavor.

2. Use a pin or a similarly small, sharp tool to remove the eyes and quills from inside the body cavity of the squid.

3. Line a serving dish with the sauce, place the squid over it and top with the strips of *yuzu* citrus and lime rind.

OUTSIDE JAPAN, WE CAN ONLY GET preboiled fairy squid. In May and June, however, fresh fairy squid is available from some Japanese markets in the United States if you ask for it specially.

"I HAVE SEVERAL *SANSHO* TREES in my garden to use in my cooking and also as a sushi garnish. The special peppery bouquet of this summery plant is redolent of the season itself for me."

FISH, FISH, FISH

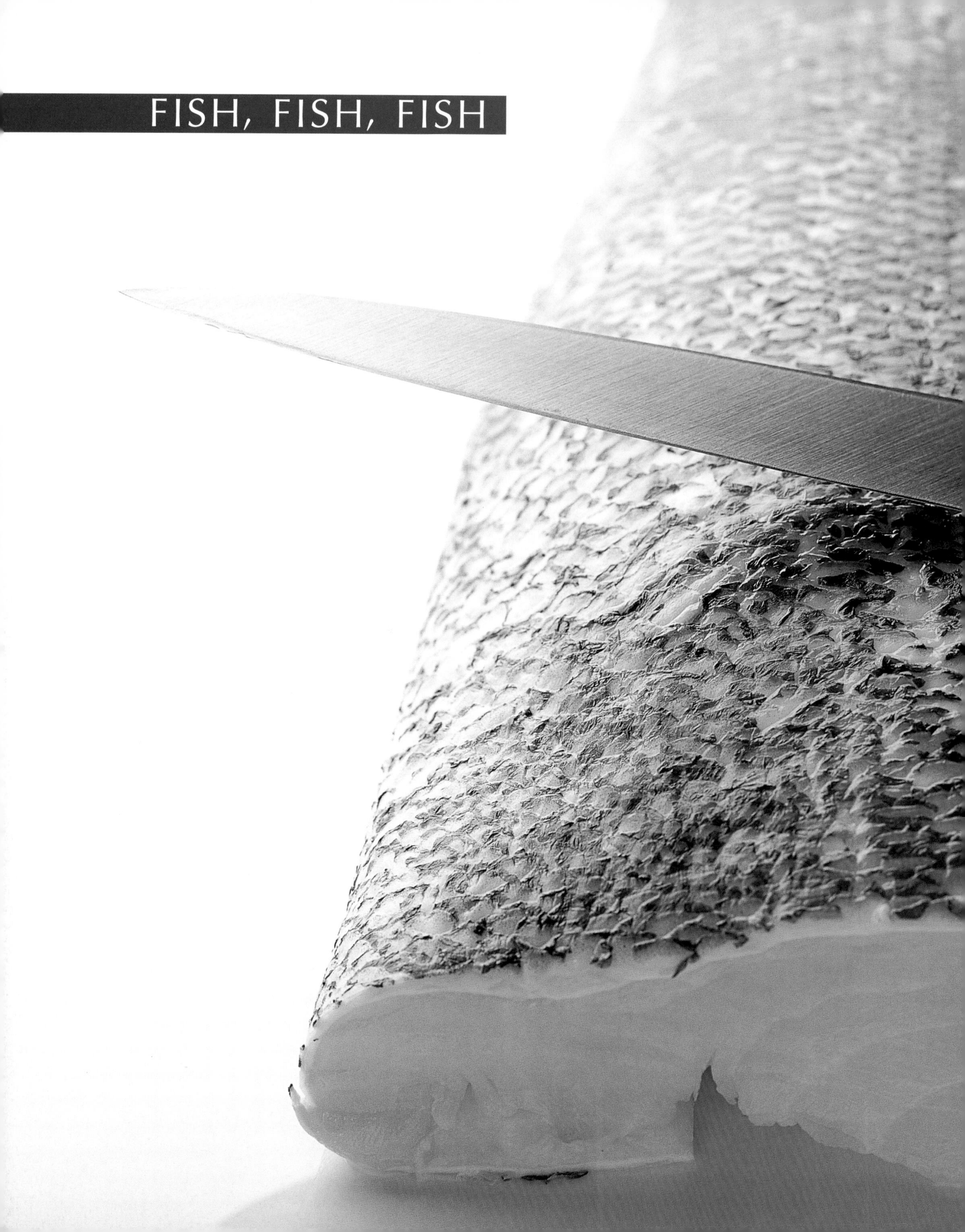

Monkfish is a winter fish whose liver is prized as a great—and therefore expensive—delicacy in Japan. At the Tsukiji fish market in Tokyo, monkfish are sold with their bellies cut open and their much sought-after livers on display. And necessarily so, too: The size of the liver determines the price of this fish. But that's not to say the rest of the fish goes to waste. In the one-pot stew, *anko-nabe*, monkfish meat, skin and liver are all simmered in *dashi* made from monkfish bones.

About the time I opened Matsuhisa in Los Angeles, I came across fresh monkfish liver on sale at a local fishmonger. Surprised, to say the least, at finding such a quintessential Japanese delicacy available in the United States, I didn't hesitate to prepare it in the traditional Japanese style. A sushi chef invariably serves monkfish liver steamed with either a *su-miso* or *ponzu* (page 174) sauce and rarely as a sushi topping. Steaming the liver produces a soft and expansive texture, not unlike the more familiar foie gras. I call it pâté, and some customers have dubbed it "ocean foie gras." My recipes are constantly evolving. I add some caviar to steamed monkfish liver, caviar not to be eaten with a knife and fork in the French fashion but with a pair of chopsticks. Monkfish Pâté with Caviar and Mustard Su-miso Sauce (page 98) is now a popular fixture on my menu.

I also include two recipes using monkfish meat, which while not exactly light like many fish, is not oily either. Expect a full-bodied, meaty texture. In Cilantro Soup with Monkfish (page 100), chunks of fish—dusted in arrowroot and deep-fried—are added to a *dashi*-based soup flavored with a little cilantro to create a refreshing new taste. The arrowroot absorbs liquid from the soup, giving the fish a light, delicate coating. For Baked Monkfish Medley with Tosa-zu (page 102), the meat, skin and liver are served with the tangy Tosa-zu sauce (page 173), which derives its name from the ancient province of Tosa on the island of Shikoku. This sauce usually accompanies Tosa's famous *tataki*—a style of sashimi in which fish (usually bonito) fillets are seared on the surface, sliced and topped with finely chopped white scallions and ginger.

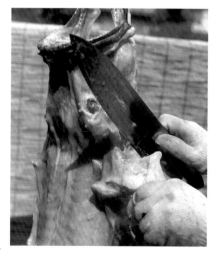

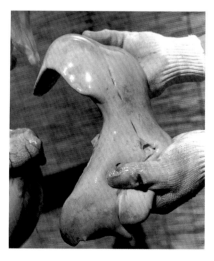

CHILEAN SEA BASS

Everyone seems to like the rich, defined flavor of this big fish from Chile. The four recipes included here (pages 106 to 113) will work with other fish that have a high fat content, such as salmon and black cod. Indeed, these were my staple fish for grilling and sautéing until about ten years ago when I discovered a fellow chef using Chilean sea bass at a charity function. It was an epiphany for me to find another fish that retained its soft juiciness after cooking. The idea of working with new or unfamiliar ingredients genuinely excites me and I lost no time in placing an order for Chilean sea bass with my fishmonger. Whims and fancies may well inspire the debut of a new food at Matsuhisa or any of my other restaurants, but it is my customers who ultimately decide what stays on the menu. Chilean sea bass is currently available in all eleven of my restaurants in four countries.

WHITE FISH

On my menu you will see many different kinds of white fish, primarily red snapper, flounder, sea bass and grouper. Personally, I like such fish served as sushi and sashimi. The Peruvian-influenced ceviche (page 118) and tiradito (page 120) and the hot-oil-drizzled New Style Sashimi (page 116)—my three trademark sashimi dishes—have completely revolutionized the tired image of sashimi by turning on its head the Japanese convention of only serving raw fish with grated *wasabi* and soy sauce.

For those who are put off by the idea of eating fish raw—perhaps because they mistakenly believe that raw fish smells—I recommend they try my New Style Sashimi first, as it is partially cooked. Next they should try the diverting spiciness of ceviche. Finally they should tackle the simple freshness of tiradito. After all, eating fresh fish raw is a great treat.

TORO

Occasionally at the fish market I come across such an excellent specimen of tuna that the fish seems to be crying out to me to buy it whole. But, as I take pride in only serving the very best ingredients in peak condition, the amount of sushi and sashimi that can be made from one whole tuna is actually quite limited. So I sear parts of it like a rare steak—sizzling on the outside and raw on the inside, with an impressive "melt-in-the-mouth" texture. My Toro Steak is introduced here with Wakame Su-miso Sauce (page 134), but is equally delightful with my versatile Wasabi Pepper Sauce (page 173) or pungent Spicy Lemon Garlic Sauce (page 172), especially when served with plain short-grain rice. Many Japanese, including myself, would naturally have some resistance to "wasting" a fillet of *toro* by not serving it raw. Fortunately, however, my American customers are free from such prejudices and are able to enjoy the *toro* steak on its own terms.

As a creative chef, I can never be satisfied with making the same dishes day in and day out. Evolution and change are essential to my success and go hand-in-hand with a desire to serve customers meals they will enjoy and never forget. Encouraged by regulars who always ask me for something different, I have become bold enough to recommend new styles of *toro* cooking—such as Toro Toban Yaki (page 128)—to other customers who usually take their *toro* as sushi or sashimi. After all, it is part of my mission as a chef to present my guests with new and appetizing tastes and experiences.

Returning to my whole tuna: I am still left with various scraps of meat—including the stringy yet tasty parts from the head and the tail—that can't be used for sushi, sashimi or steak. True, I could make a sushi roll out of them. Instead, I tuck the scraps away in the freezer and nearly forget about them. A thin layer of ice has developed on the surface of the *toro*; its fat content has prevented further freezing. Perfectly complemented by the salty taste of caviar, a chilled sauce made with *wasabi*, soy sauce and *dashi*, along with a glass of champagne, a new à la carte dish—Toro Tartare with Caviar (page 132)—is born.

MONKFISH PÂTÉ WITH CAVIAR AND MUSTARD SU-MISO SAUCE

DISCOVER THE RICH FLAVOR AND FOIE-GRAS-LIKE TEXTURE OF STEAMED MONKFISH LIVER IN THIS VARIATION ON A JAPANESE STANDARD, WITH THE ADDITION OF CAVIAR AND A MISO-BASED SAUCE CONTAINING JAPANESE MUSTARD AND RICE VINEGAR.

INGREDIENTS — serves 4

7 ounces (200g) monkfish liver

¾ cup (160ml) Mustard Su-miso Sauce (page 172)

4 tablespoons osetra caviar

bayberries and *menegi* for garnish, optional

flowers for garnish, optional

METHOD

1. Remove the blood vessels from the monkfish liver with a knife and peel off the thin membrane.

2. Soak the liver in salted water for 20 to 30 minutes. (The salt-to-water ratio should be 3% salt to water, or 1 ounce [30g] salt to 1 quart [1l] of water.) Pat dry with a paper towel.

3. Place the liver on a sheet of plastic wrap and roll into a cylindrical shape about 2 inches (5cm) in diameter. Use a bamboo skewer to poke air holes in the wrap to allow any liquid to drain during steaming. Next roll the liver up even more securely in aluminum foil. Tighten the foil at both ends. Then wrap the liver package in a bamboo rolling mat and secure with a rubber band to hold the shape.

4. Steam on a rack over simmering water for 40 to 45 minutes. Set aside to cool at room temperature, then chill in the refrigerator.

5. Cut the chilled liver into 4 disks. Put a large spoonful of Mustard Su-miso Sauce on each of 4 plates and place a piece of liver on top. Garnish with a dollop of caviar and some *menegi* and decorate with a bayberry and a flower.

I WOULD ALSO RECOMMEND MONKFISH PÂTÉ with finely chopped white scallions (spring onions) and *ponzu* (page 174).

CILANTRO SOUP WITH MONKFISH

CHUNKS OF MONKFISH—DUSTED IN ARROWROOT AND DEEP-FRIED—ARE ADDED TO A *DASHI*-BASED SOUP FLAVORED WITH CILANTRO TO CREATE A REFRESHING NEW TASTE.

INGREDIENTS ——————————————————————— serves 4

Soup

2 ¼ cups (440ml) Dashi (page 174)

2 teaspoons saké

2 teaspoons light soy sauce

¼ teaspoon sea salt

9 ounces (250g) monkfish

sea salt

freshly ground black pepper

vegetable oil for deep-frying

arrowroot starch for dusting

1 teaspoon finely chopped cilantro (coriander) leaves

menegi and thin slices of lime for garnish

METHOD

1. Make the soup: Bring the *dashi* to a boil in a medium saucepan over high heat. Add the saké and light soy sauce, and adjust the flavor with sea salt.

2. Slice the monkfish into pieces about ½ inch (1 cm) thick, and sprinkle with a little sea salt and black pepper.

3. Bring about 3 inches (8 cm) of oil in a medium saucepan to 340°–350°F (170°–180°C). Dust the monkfish pieces with arrowroot and deep-fry for 3 to 4 minutes until crisp. Drain on paper towels.

4. Arrange the monkfish pieces in 4 soup dishes. Add the cilantro to the soup and pour into the dishes. Garnish with *menegi* and lime. Serve immediately.

MAKE SURE YOU ADD THE MONKFISH when it is freshly fried and still hot.

BAKED MONKFISH MEDLEY WITH TOSA-ZU

Monkfish MEAT, SKIN and LIVER are topped with a GENEROUS sprinkling of *ASATSUKI* chives and served with TANGY *Tosa-zu* sauce.

INGREDIENTS ———————————————————— serves 4

vegetable oil for deep-frying

1 ¾ ounces (50g) monkfish skin

3 ½ ounces (100g) monkfish

1 ¾ ounces (50g) monkfish liver

sea salt

freshly ground black pepper

4 cloves elephant (or regular) garlic, thinly sliced

10 *asatsuki* chives, sliced into thin rounds

pink peppercorns

1 cup (200ml) Tosa-zu (page 173)

METHOD

1. Bring about 3 inches (8cm) of oil in a small saucepan to 355°F (180°C). Cut the monkfish skin into 1-inch (2–3-cm) squares and deep-fry for 2 to 3 minutes. Set aside.

2. Cut the monkfish and liver into 1-inch (2–3-cm) chunks.

3. Preheat the oven to 390°F (200°C, gas 6). Sprinkle a little sea salt and black pepper over the monkfish, liver and skin. Alternate layers of the monkfish, liver, skin and finally the monkfish again in an ovenproof mold 2 ½ inches (6.5cm) in diameter.

4. Bake for 5 to 6 minutes, then top with the thinly sliced elephant garlic and bake 2 to 3 minutes more.

5. Place the mold on a serving dish, top with *asatsuki* chives and peppercorns, and then remove the mold. Pour the Tosa-zu into the dish.

OUR RESTAURANTS ALSO SERVE Salmon Skin Salad with Tosa-zu.

CHILEAN SEA BASS WITH NOBU'S BLACK BEAN SAUCE

RICH CHILEAN SEA BASS IS STEAMED FOR GREATER SWEETNESS WITH CHINESE BLACK BEAN SAUCE.

INGREDIENTS ──────────────────────────────────── serves 4

4 Chilean sea bass fillets, 6 ½ ounces (180g) each

sea salt

freshly ground black pepper

4 tablespoons Chinese salted black bean paste, mixed with a little saké

8 tablespoons saké

2/3 ounce (20g) ginger spears (page 174)

chives, cut into 1 ½-inch (4-cm) lengths

New Style Oil

6 tablespoons pure olive oil and 2 teaspoons sesame oil, mixed

. . .

shredded beet (beetroot) and finely sliced *myoga* ginger for garnish

METHOD

1. Sprinkle each fillet with a little sea salt and black pepper and then spread with the black bean paste.

2. Place the fish in a heatproof dish, add saké and steam for 10 minutes over high heat in a steamer. Remove the dish from the steamer and pour the accumulated cooking liquid onto 4 deep plates for serving.

3. Top the fish with the ginger spears and chives. Heat the New Style Oil in a small frying pan until just before it begins to smoke, then pour it over the fish.

4. Transfer the fish to the plates containing the reserved steaming liquid. Garnish with the beet and *myoga* ginger.

STEAMING ON HIGH HEAT SEALS in the juices of fresh fish.

"I FIRST CAME ACROSS THE TECHNIQUE OF DRIZZLING HOT OIL OVER STEAMED FISH through Peruvian home-cooking. Instead of Chilean sea bass, I used a gelatinous Peruvian fish called *pejesapo* (toad-fish) that has delicious, melt-in-the-mouth flesh. This recipe works well with any fatty fish, as it really brings out the inherent sweetness."

CHILEAN SEA BASS WITH SPICY MOROMI MISO

WITH NO OTHER SEASONING, THE FISH IS STEEPED IN *MOROMI MISO* ENHANCED BY THE KICK OF JALAPEÑO.

INGREDIENTS ——————————————————————— serves 4

2 jalapeños

3 cups (750g) *moromi miso*, plus more for garnish

4 Chilean sea bass fillets, 6 ½ ounces (180g) each

4 cucumbers, thinly sliced lengthwise

cucumber flowers for garnish, optional

1 stalk *hajikami* (page 174) per serving

METHOD

1. Mince the jalapeño and mix well with the *moromi miso*.

2. Pat the fillets dry with paper towels. Slather the fish on all sides with the *moromi miso* and place in a nonreactive dish or bowl and cover tightly with plastic wrap. Leave to steep in the refrigerator for 2 to 3 days.

3. Preheat the oven to 400°F (200°C, gas 6). Preheat a grill or broiler. Lightly wipe off any excess *moromi miso* clinging to the fillets but don't rinse it off. Place the fish on the grill, or in a broiler pan, and grill or broil until the surface of the fish turns brown. Then bake for 10 to 15 minutes in the oven.

4. For each serving, lay the thin slices of cucumber on a plate and top with the baked fish. Put a dollop of *moromi miso* on top of a decoratively cut cucumber chunk and place it next to the fish. Garnish with a cucumber flower and *hajikami*.

THE FISH SHOULD BE PATTED DRY THOROUGHLY before being covered with the *moromi miso*. Grilling it lightly releases a delicious toasted aroma.

"FOR CENTURIES, THE JAPANESE HAVE PRESERVED FISH by pickling and curing. Nowadays, fish is still pickled in *miso*, saké lees (the dregs left over from the saké brewing process) or soy sauce. Black Cod with Miso (page 124), one such pickled dish, was already popular in my restaurants, so I came up with this recipe using a different fish and offering a different flavor through the spicy addition of jalapeño."

CHILEAN SEA BASS AND TRUFFLES WITH YUZU SOY BUTTER SAUCE

AN EXQUISITE EAST-MEETS-WEST COMBINATION: BAKED CHILEAN SEA BASS IS TOPPED WITH TRUFFLES AND SERVED WITH A SAUCE OF BUTTER, SOY SAUCE AND *YUZU*.

INGREDIENTS ————————————————————————— serves 4

sea salt

4 fiddlehead ferns for garnish, optional

1/2 cup (100ml) Dashi (page 174)

1 teaspoon light soy sauce

4 Chilean sea bass fillets, 6 1/2 ounces (180g) each

freshly ground black pepper

1 tablespoon vegetable oil

4 garlic stalks, cut into 5-inch (13-cm) lengths for garnish, optional

4 tablespoons clarified butter (page 173)

1 3/4 ounces (50g) fresh black truffles, finely sliced

truffle oil

Yuzu soy sauce

2 tablespoons plus 1 teaspoon *yuzu* juice and 5 tablespoons plus 2 teaspoons soy sauce, mixed

· · ·

1 sheet of bamboo shoot skin for garnish, optional

METHOD

1. Bring a small pot of water to a boil and add a pinch of sea salt. Boil the fiddlehead ferns for 2 to 3 minutes. Drain. Mix the *dashi* and soy sauce and add the fiddlehead ferns. Set aside for about 1 hour.

2. Preheat the oven to 475°F (250°C, gas 9). Sprinkle the fillets with a little sea salt and black pepper. Bake for 10 minutes and place on individual plates.

3. Heat the oil in a small frying pan over high heat and fry the garlic stalks for 30 seconds. Set aside.

4. Heat the clarified butter in a small saucepan. Lay the truffle slices on the fillets so they overlap like fish scales. Drizzle the truffle oil and clarified butter over the fish. Spoon the *yuzu* soy sauce around the fish and garnish with the bamboo shoot skin, fiddlehead ferns and garlic stalks.

THE TANG OF *YUZU* IS A GREAT FOIL for fatty fish like Chilean sea bass.

HERB-GRILLED CHILEAN SEA BASS WITH FRIED SOY BEAN CURD

TRY THIS JUICY FISH TOGETHER WITH CRISP-FRIED *YUBA* FOR THEIR CONTRASTING TEXTURES.

INGREDIENTS ——————————————————————— serves 4

vegetable oil for deep-frying

4 large (10-inch- [24-cm-] square) sheets dried *yuba*

finely chopped parsley leaves (enough to completely cover the fish)

3 tablespoons extra virgin olive oil

shichimi togarashi to taste

4 Chilean sea bass fillets, 6 ½ ounces (180g) each

sea salt

freshly ground black pepper

½ cup (100ml) soy sauce

½ cup (100ml) lemon juice

red smartweed for garnish, optional

METHOD

1. Bring 1 inch (2.5 cm) of oil in a deep, 12-inch (30-cm) frying pan to 355°F (180°C). Fry the *yuba* sheets, one at a time, until crisp. Fry with care, as they burn easily. Drain and place the fried *yuba* on individual plates.

2. Combine the parsley with the olive oil. Add *shichimi togarashi* to taste. Set aside.

3. Preheat the oven to 475°F (250°C, gas 9). Sprinkle the fillets with a little sea salt and black pepper and bake for 8 to 9 minutes. (The fish will be about 80% cooked through.) Top with the parsley and oil mixture and cook for 2 to 3 minutes more, without charring the parsley.

4. Arrange the fish on top of the *yuba* and drizzle the soy sauce and lemon juice over all. Sprinkle with the red smartweed.

I USE PARSLEY IN THIS DISH, but you can try cilantro (coriander) or other herbs of your own choosing.

"*YUBA* IS THE THIN FILM THAT FORMS ON THE SURFACE OF SOY MILK WHEN HEATED. Outside Japan, it is usually only available in its dried form. Apart from this dish, my restaurants serve *yuba* wrapped around shrimp and deep-fried."

NEW STYLE SASHIMI

WHITE FISH SASHIMI IS DRIZZLED WITH SOY SAUCE AND *YUZU* JUICE, THEN A HOT OIL MIXTURE
IS POURED OVER IT TO CREATE A NEW STYLE OF SASHIMI. TRY IT WITH SHELLFISH, BEEF OR TOFU.

INGREDIENTS ——————————————————————————————————— serves 4

18 ounces (500g) red snapper fillet

1 teaspoon finely grated garlic

ginger spears from 1 knob of ginger
(page 174)

menegi or chives

2 teaspoons white sesame seeds, toasted

Yuzu soy sauce

1 tablespoon plus 1 teaspoon *yuzu*
juice and 3 tablespoons plus 1
teaspoon soy sauce, combined

• • •

carrot curl (page 174) for garnish

New Style Oil

6 tablespoons pure olive oil and 2
teaspoons sesame oil, combined

METHOD

1. Cut the fish into paper-thin slices using the *usu-zukuri*
   cutting technique (page 19).

2. Arrange the fish slices on a serving plate. On each slice
   dab a little grated garlic and place ginger spears and a
   few *menegi* or chives. Sprinkle the sesame seeds over
   the fish. Drizzle the *yuzu* soy sauce over the top and garnish with the carrot curl.

3. Just prior to serving, heat the New Style Oil in a small
   frying pan until just before it begins to smoke. Pour it
   over the fish slices and serve.

RECOMMENDED FOR HESITANT SASHIMI NOVICES.

"ONE DAY, A MATSUHISA REGULAR REFUSED

SOME WHITE FISH SASHIMI because she couldn't eat raw fish. I
wanted to somehow salvage the dish that I'd spent time slicing and arranging. A pan of heated olive oil in the kitchen
inspired me. I drizzled the fish with *ponzu* and spooned over
hot oil to cook it partially. I begged my customer to give it
another try: She ended up eating every scrap of my first
serving of New Style Sashimi."

SEAFOOD CEVICHE, NOBU STYLE

THE CEVICHE I LEARNED TO MAKE IN PERU IS THE ULTIMATE NOBU FARE, MY ABSOLUTE FAVORITE. A COMBINATION OF RAW AND COOKED SEAFOOD, VEGETABLES AND SPICY-SOUR CEVICHE SAUCE, THIS DISH IS GREAT FOR A HOT SUMMER.

INGREDIENTS ———————————————————— serves 4

6½ ounces (180g) seafood (delicate-flavored varieties such as fresh white fish and shellfish, boiled octopus, boiled squid, boiled shrimp), cut into bite-size pieces

4 teaspoons finely chopped cilantro (coriander) leaves

¼ red onion, thinly sliced

½ cucumber, peeled and cut into thin round slices

4 each red, yellow and orange mini tomatoes, halved

5 tablespoons plus 1 teaspoon Ceviche Sauce (page 170)

cilantro sprigs for garnish

METHOD

Mix all the seafood and vegetables together well. Combine with Ceviche Sauce and transfer to a serving dish. Top with a cilantro sprig.

CEVICHE AND BEER IS A MATCH MADE IN HEAVEN! One of our most popular dishes, it's especially tempting in the summer when appetites fade a little.

"A STYLE OF SASHIMI FAR REMOVED FROM THE JAPANESE IDEA, CEVICHE is a typical Latin American dish believed to have originated in Peru. Ceviche has now become my signature dish and a popular fixture on the Matsuhisa menu. It was a different story when I first opened Nobu in New York: Hardly anyone knew what ceviche was.

I was pleasantly surprised when I first encountered this 'Peruvian sashimi' at a ceviche restaurant in Lima, which served plates of spicy, sour ceviche with palate-cleansing boiled corn and potatoes on the side.

We mix fresh fish with Ceviche Sauce to order, rather than pre-marinating, which destroys the flavor of seafood and robs white fish of its attractive translucence.

Besides this seafood ceviche, our other popular variations include a lobster ceviche, a ceviche wrapped in limestone lettuce leaves and, for those leery of seafood, we even have a tomato ceviche (page 152). Ceviche is a special dish that can be made from the seafood morsels left over from sushi and sashimi."

WHITE FISH TIRADITO, NOBU STYLE

LIKE CEVICHE, TIRADITO IS A FOOD I ENCOUNTERED IN PERU AND THEN ADAPTED IN MY OWN WAY TO CREATE A NOBU MASTERPIECE! HERE SASHIMI IS EATEN WITH SEA SALT AND THE TANG OF LEMON AND *YUZU* JUICE. PERUVIAN CHILI PASTE ADDS BITE TO IT.

INGREDIENTS ————————————————————————————— serves 4

18 ounces (500g) red snapper fillet

rocoto chili paste

cilantro (coriander) leaves, stems removed

1 tablespoon plus 1 teaspoon *yuzu* juice

2 tablespoons plus 2 teaspoons lemon juice

sea salt

METHOD

1. Cut the fish into paper-thin slices using the *usu-zukuri* cutting technique (page 19).

2. Fan out the fish slices on a serving dish. Add a small dollop of rocoto chili paste on each slice and put the cilantro leaves at the center. Drizzle the *yuzu* and lemon juice over all.

3. Sprinkle with sea salt to taste. The flavor of this dish depends on the salt, so if too little is used it will taste bland.

EATING THE FISH PIECES TOGETHER with the cilantro is a must. Other chili pastes can be substituted for rocoto.

"TIRADITO DIFFERS FROM CEVICHE IN THAT IT CONTAINS NO ONIONS. In the original South American dish, cut fish is 'thrown' (*tirar* in Spanish) into a bowl and mixed with ceviche seasonings. In my version I use the *usu-zukuri* cutting technique to 'paste' paper-thin slices of fish attractively onto a plate. As a trained sushi chef, I know how important presentation is; but rather than spend ages mulling over the look of a dish, I prefer to spring a surprise arrangement that I hope my customers will appreciate."

SOLE WITH SPICY BLACK BEAN SAUCE

SOLE IS SMEARED WITH BLACK BEANS AND CHILI BEAN SAUCE, THEN STEAMED. HEATED NEW STYLE OIL IS THEN POURED OVER THE FISH. THE KEY ELEMENTS ARE THE TASTE AND AROMA OF THE BLACK BEANS, PLUS THE KICK OF CHILI BEAN SAUCE.

INGREDIENTS —————————————————————————————— serves 4

2 sole, about 9–11 ounces (250–300g) each

sea salt

freshly ground black pepper

5 tablespoons plus 1 teaspoon saké

2 tablespoons Chinese salted black bean paste

1 tablespoon Chinese chili bean sauce

New Style Oil

6 tablespoons pure olive oil and 2 teaspoons sesame oil, combined

. . .

ginger spears from 1 knob of ginger (page 174)

1 ½ ounces (40g) onion sprouts

hamabofu leaves (page 33) for garnish, optional

METHOD

1. Skin and filet the fish, keeping the bones intact. Wind the bones into a ring and deep-fry until crisp.

2. Arrange the fillets on a heatproof dish. Season with a little sea salt and black pepper and sprinkle with the saké. Spread the black bean paste and chili bean sauce all over the fish. Steam over high heat for 7 to 8 minutes.

3. Combine the New Style Oil ingredients. Remove the dish from the steamer and pour a little of the accumulated cooking liquid onto individual plates. Top the fish with the ginger spears and onion sprouts. Heat the New Style Oil in a small frying pan until just before it begins to smoke. Pour the hot oil over the fish.

4. Place the fillets on the plates containing the cooking liquid. Garnish with the fried bone rings and *hamabofu*.

THIS IS A BIG HIT IN THE LONDON RESTAURANT, where we use Dover sole. The firm flesh of Dover sole makes it one of my favorites.

BLACK COD WITH MISO

Black cod is steeped in SWEET *MISO* before being baked in the oven. The sweetness of NOBU-STYLE Saikyo Miso is an EXCELLENT match with the PLUMPNESS of the fish.

INGREDIENTS ———————————————————————————— serves 4

4 black cod fillets, about ½ pound (230g) each

3 cups (800g) Nobu-style Saikyo Miso (page 172)

1 stalk *hajikami* (page 174) per serving

METHOD

1. Pat the fillets thoroughly dry with paper towels. Slather the fish with Nobu-style Saikyo Miso and place in a nonreactive dish or bowl and cover tightly with plastic wrap. Leave to steep in the refrigerator for 2 to 3 days.

2. Preheat the oven to 400°F (200°C, gas 6). Preheat a grill or broiler. Lightly wipe off any excess *miso* clinging to the fillets but don't rinse it off. Place the fish on the grill, or in a broiler pan, and grill or broil until the surface of the fish turns brown. Then bake for 10 to 15 minutes.

3. Arrange the black cod fillets on individual plates and garnish with *hajikami*. Add a few extra drops of Nobu-style Saikyo Miso to each plate.

THIS IS A FAVORITE OF ROBERT DE NIRO'S, who often eats it with saké in hand. This recipe also works for beef, *toro* and salmon.

TORO TOBAN YAKI

TORO SIZZLING ON A HOT PLATE IN FRONT OF YOUR EYES AROUSES THE
APPETITE. IT IS SERVED WITH THREE KINDS OF MUSHROOMS.

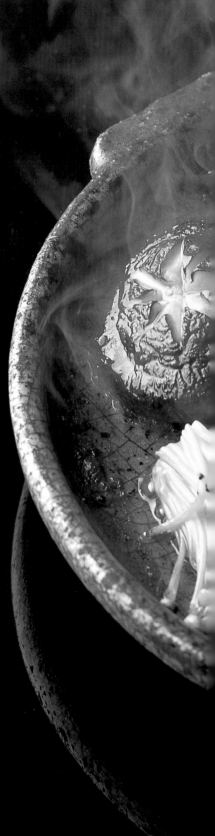

INGREDIENTS —————————————————————————————— serves 4

4 *toro* fillets, 3 ½ ounces (100g) each
sea salt
freshly ground black pepper
4 teaspoons finely grated garlic
4 *shiitake* mushrooms, stems removed
7 ounces (200g) tiny green asparagus
4 broccoli florets, cut into bite-size pieces

7 ounces (200g) *enoki* mushrooms
3 ounces (80g) *maitake* mushrooms
8 tablespoons clarified butter (page 173)
8 tablespoons saké
4 tablespoons soy sauce
4 tablespoons *yuzu* juice

METHOD

1. Preheat a barbecue, grill or griddle pan. Preheat a *toban* ceramic hot plate on high heat.

2. Sprinkle the *toro* fillets with a little sea salt and black pepper and spread with the grated garlic. Sear the surface of each side of the fish fillets on the grill until they are white. Also grill the *shiitake* briefly on high heat.

3. Bring a medium saucepan of water to a boil and add a pinch of sea salt. Parboil the asparagus and broccoli, then plunge them briefly into iced water. Drain.

4. Spread the clarified butter on the *toban* and add the *toro*, vegetables and mushrooms. Pour the saké and soy sauce over them, followed by the *yuzu* juice. Do this quickly so the *toro* doesn't overcook. Turn off heat, cover and serve.

MAKE SURE YOU EAT THIS DISH IMMEDIATELY. Heat from the *toban* ceramic plate will continue to cook the fish.

A *TOBAN* IS A CERAMIC DISH WITH A LID, often used in Japan to prepare food directly in front of a diner.

TORO WITH JALAPEÑO

IN THIS DISH, *TORO* SASHIMI IS PEPPED UP WITH JALAPEÑO. SEARING THE *TORO*'S SURFACE BRINGS OUT A ROASTED AROMA AND ALTERS THE FLAVOR. A SAUCE OF SOY SAUCE AND *YUZU* JUICE IS DRIZZLED OVER THE *TORO* AS A FINISHING TOUCH.

INGREDIENTS ———————————————————————————— serves 4

4 *toro* fillets, 3 ½ ounces (100g) each

4 sheets *okiuto*, optional

1 teaspoon finely grated garlic

cilantro (coriander) leaves, stems removed

2 jalapeños, sliced into thin rounds

Yuzu soy sauce

8 tablespoons *yuzu* juice and 4 tablespoons soy sauce, mixed

METHOD

1. Slice the *toro* as thinly as possible, about ⅛ inch (3–4 mm) thick.

2. Sear the surface of the *toro* with a propane torch (blow torch). Alternatively, grill the *toro* briefly over high heat.

3. Line 4 plates with the *okiuto* and arrange the *toro* over it. Top each *toro* slice with a dab of grated garlic, a cilantro leaf and a jalapeño round. Pour the *yuzu* soy sauce around.

THIS IS A POPULAR DISH IN OUR RESTAURANTS when served with *hamachi*. The flavors involved lend themselves well to fatty fish.

"I FIRST MADE THIS WITH *HAMACHI* AS A SNACK AFTER A CHARITY EVENT. I'd wanted to make tiradito, but as no chili paste was left I covered the fish with sliced jalapeño instead."

TORO TARTARE WITH CAVIAR

Minced *TORO* is CHILLED and mixed with onion and garlic. The tartare is DRESSED with soy sauce, *WASABI* and *DASHI* and CROWNED with CAVIAR.

INGREDIENTS ———————————————————————————— serves 4

Sauce

4 tablespoons Dashi (page 174)

1 tablespoon plus 1 teaspoon soy sauce

4 tablespoons Wasabi Pepper Sauce (page 173)

8 ½ ounces (240g) *toro* fillet

2 teaspoons finely chopped onion

1 teaspoon finely grated garlic

4 teaspoons osetra caviar

menegi for garnish

sprig of plum blossom and bamboo shoot skin for garnish, optional

METHOD

1. Make the sauce: Add the *dashi* and soy sauce to the Wasabi Pepper Sauce and refrigerate.

2. Mince the *toro* as finely as possible and spread it loosely on a plate. Put the plate in the freezer for 10 to 15 minutes.

3. Working quickly, remove the *toro* from the freezer and combine with the onion and garlic. Stuff the mixture into 4 2-inch- (5-cm-) diameter metal molds each on a chilled serving dish and then remove molds.

4. Top the *toro* with caviar and *menegi* and pour the sauce on carefully so as not to disturb the arrangement. Garnish with a sprig of plum blossom and bamboo shoot skin.

THE KEY HERE IS CHILLING THE SERVING PLATE, and chilling the tartare to the point, preferably, where a faint layer of ice forms over its surface. You can make an equally good tartare this way with *hamachi*, salmon or red tuna.

TORO STEAK WITH WAKAME MUSTARD SU-MISO SAUCE

JAPANESE USUALLY THINK OF SASHIMI OR SUSHI WHEN THEY HEAR THE WORD *TORO*, BUT HERE I TRIED SEARING IT, STEAK-STYLE. THE SEAWEED IN THE MUSTARD SU-MISO SAUCE ADDS A HINT OF THE SEASHORE.

INGREDIENTS ———————————————————————————— serves 4

Sauce

¾ cup plus 1 tablespoon (160ml) Mustard Su-miso Sauce (page 172)

¾ cup (80g) roughly chopped fresh *wakame*

4 *toro* fillets, 3½ ounces (100g) each

sea salt

freshly ground black pepper

2 teaspoons finely grated garlic

sansho sprigs for garnish, optional

40 *udo* curls (page 174) for garnish, optional

METHOD

1. Make the sauce: Blend the Mustard Su-miso Sauce and *wakame* in a food processor until the seaweed is finely shredded.

2. Preheat a barbecue, grill or griddle pan. Sprinkle the *toro* filets with a little sea salt and black pepper, and dab with the grated garlic. Briefly sear both sides of the *toro*.

3. Spread the sauce over the middle of 4 plates. Cut the fillets into bite-size pieces and arrange them over the sauce. Top with *sansho* sprigs and *udo* curls.

"TOGETHER WITH *NORI* AND *KONBU*, WAKAME IS ONE OF THE MOST POPULAR AND widely used seaweeds in Japan, where seaweed is believed to be good for your health and the secret to a long life. But in many other countries, things like *wakame*, *nori* and *konbu* are lumped together and considered just a useless weed growing in the sea. I like seaweed, so I serve it in salad and hope it catches on more worldwide."

FRESHWATER EEL AND SEA EEL

In Japan, freshwater eel is eaten for a nutritive boost in the dog days of summer when one's energy sags in the heat. I have freshwater eel flown in from Japan and prepare it *kabayaki*-style, where the eel is steamed, broiled and basted with a sweet sauce, and served over rice for lunch. Freshwater Eel and Foie Gras (page 138) combines the sumptuousness of foie gras with that of a sweet sauce, making it the richest recipe in this book. Sometimes we should indulge ourselves!

Although the sushi chef generally restricts himself to raw seafood, eel and vinegared *ayu* sweetfish are two notable exceptions in his repertoire. Sea eel is indispensable on the sushi menu and in tempura, too, which wouldn't be quite the same without it. Aside from sushi, sea eel can be served *kabayaki*-style like its freshwater cousin or with *wasabi* soy sauce. I like it deep-fried and sprinkled with curry powder and salt.

How to make freshwater and sea eel bone crackers

Wash away any meat left on the bone. Wind the bone into a ring and let it dry in well-ventilated shade for a whole day and night. Deep-fry in vegetable oil until crisp.

FILETING EEL

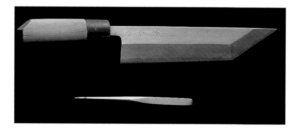

1. Stick an ice pick through the head of the eel to fix it to the chopping board.

2. Make a cut from the base of the neck toward the tail, keeping the edge of the knife on the backbone.

3. Open the eel and remove the backbone by cutting underneath it toward the tail.

4. Discard the internal organs. Cut off the tail and fins.

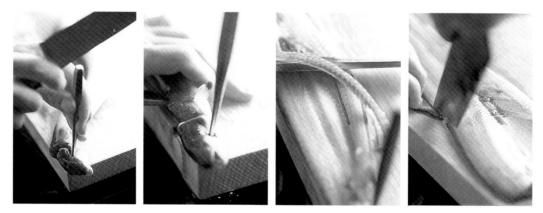

FRESHWATER EEL AND FOIE GRAS

I COMBINED FOIE GRAS WITH FRESHWATER EEL BECAUSE THEY BOTH GO WELL WITH A
SWEET SAUCE. THIS SUMPTUOUS DISH IS FINISHED OFF WITH A THICK REDUCTION OF
SOY SAUCE AND *MIRIN*.

INGREDIENTS
serves 4

2 freshwater eels, about 18 ounces (500g) each

saké

8 disks of *daikon*, about ¾ inch (2cm) thick

1 cup (200ml) Dashi (page 174)

1 tablespoon light soy sauce

4 *shiitake* mushrooms, stems removed

vegetable oil for deep-frying

4 *shiso* leaves

sea salt

freshly ground black pepper

4 pieces foie gras, about 1 ½ ounces (40g) each

Sauce

½ cup (100ml) soy sauce

1 ½ cups (300ml) *mirin*

truffle oil

. . .

4 eel bone crackers (page 136)

METHOD

1. Filet the eels (page 136). Rinse and drain.

2. Preheat the oven to 475°F (250°C, gas 9). Place the eels in a baking dish. Sprinkle the surface of the eels with saké and bake for 5 minutes on each side so that they cook evenly.

3. Cut the eels into 4 equal pieces, place in a heatproof dish and steam over high heat for 20 minutes. This tenderizes the meat.

4. Bring a small saucepan of water to a boil and add the *daikon*. Boil the *daikon* until tender, then remove and steep in the *dashi* to which the light soy sauce has been added.

5. Preheat a grill or broiler. Lightly grill the *shiitake* mushrooms. Set aside.

6. Deep-fry the *shiso* leaves.

7. Sprinkle a little sea salt and black pepper on the foie gras. Heat a medium frying pan over medium heat. Add a very thin coat of oil (just enough to prevent the foie gras from burning) and sauté the foie gras pieces on medium heat until both sides are brown. After about 2 minutes in the pan, touch the foie gras with a finger. Remove the foie gras from the pan while there is a bit of bounce left. (If overcooked, it will secrete fat, and with it an undesirable taste and smell.)

8. Make the sauce: Add soy sauce and *mirin* to the frying pan in which the foie gras was sautéed. Bring the sauce to boil over high heat. When the sauce thickens, turn off the heat. Add a few drops of truffle oil and the *shiitake* mushrooms, and give a quick stir.

9. On each of 4 plates, arrange 2 pieces of eel and 1 piece of foie gras on 2 disks of *daikon*. Pour the sauce over all. Top with a *shiitake* mushroom and garnish with a fried *shiso* leaf and an eel bone cracker.

DINERS HAVE ALSO LIKED THIS DISH made with Chilean sea bass instead of eel.

SEA EEL ROLL

Sea eel is encased in a thin sheet of dough with AVOCADO and flying fish roe. The rolls are eaten by first DIPPING in Tsume Sweet Sauce.

INGREDIENTS ───────────────────────────── serves 4

2 sea eels, about 3 ½ ounces (100g) each

saké

½ avocado

2 sheets pâte brique (page 63)

2 ½ tablespoons flying fish roe

4 sea eel bone crackers (page 136)

mustard leaves for garnish

4 tablespoons Tsume Sweet Sauce (page 166)

METHOD

1. Filet the eels (page 136). Rinse and drain.

2. Preheat the oven to 475°F (250°C, gas 9). Place the eels in a baking dish. Sprinkle the surface of the eels with saké and bake for 3 to 4 minutes on each side so that they cook evenly. Cut each fillet in half lengthwise and then in half crosswise.

3. Cut the avocado lengthwise into 8 equal pieces.

4. Preheat a grill or broiler. Cut the pâte brique sheets in half to form 4 semicircles. On one sheet at a time, place 1 strip of sea eel, 1 piece of avocado and some roe in the middle. Fold each side of the pâte brique one at a time over the filling, then roll up away from you. Grill or broil until crisp and slightly brown.

5. Lay the sea eel bone crackers on 4 plates, and arrange the sea eel rolls and mustard leaves on each. Garnish with a smear of Tsume Sweet Sauce to the side.

A NOVEL WAY TO SERVE THIS would be to add vinegared rice to the roll.

SALADS, VEGETABLES AND SOBA

SASHIMI SALAD WITH MATSUHISA DRESSING

A FAVORITE WITH CUSTOMERS FROM WHEN MATSUHISA FIRST OPENED, MATSUHISA DRESSING IS AN APPETIZING SOY-SAUCE-BASED MIXTURE ENHANCED BY SWEET ONIONS AND AROMATIC SESAME OIL.

INGREDIENTS ──────────────────────────────── serves 4

sea salt

freshly ground black pepper

7 ounces (200g) fresh tuna fillet

5 tablespoons plus 1 teaspoon Matsuhisa Dressing (page 171)

2 ounces (60g) assorted salad vegetables (micro greens and young bean sprouts used here)

15 *udo* curls (page 174)

red *shiso* leaves for garnish, optional

METHOD

1. Preheat a grill or broiler. Sprinkle a little sea salt and black pepper on the tuna. Briefly sear the tuna until its surface turns white. Plunge the fillet into iced water to stop it cooking any further, then shake off the excess water.

2. Pour the Matsuhisa Dressing into a serving dish. Arrange the salad vegetables, *udo* curls and red *shiso* leaves in the center of the dish. Cut the tuna into slices ⅛ inch (4–5mm) thick. Roll each slice into a cylinder and place them in a petal-like pattern around the vegetables in the center.

THIS ALL-PURPOSE DRESSING ALSO WORKS WITH MEAT, and I urge you try it on tofu as well. In the summer, I drench chilled blocks of tofu with Matsuhisa Dressing and eat it with a spoon.

SALMON SKIN SALAD WITH JALAPEÑO DRESSING

4 ounces (120g) smoked salmon skin

3 ounces (80g) assorted salad greens (*mizuna*, rocket leaves, baby spinach, mustard greens, lollo rosso lettuce, *tomyo* pea sprouts, Swiss chard used here)

1 stalk pickled *yamagobo* root, sliced

¼ cup (50ml) Jalapeño Dressing (page 171)

dried bonito flakes

METHOD

1. Grill the salmon skin until crisp, with the outer side facing the heat. Cut the skin into ⅜-inch- (1-cm-) wide strips.

2. Combine the salad greens with *yamagobo* slices and the salmon skin strips in a mixing bowl.

3. Transfer the salad to a serving dish. Pour the Jalapeño Dressing over all and top with bonito flakes.

WE ALSO SERVE THIS WITH TOSA-ZU (page 173) poured over it and plenty of bonito flakes and toasted sesame seeds.

LOBSTER SALAD WITH SPICY LEMON DRESSING

1 fresh lobster

sea salt

vegetable oil for deep-frying

2 cloves garlic, thinly sliced

5 *shiitake* mushrooms, stems removed

3 ounces (80g) assorted salad greens (*mizuna*, rocket leaves, baby spinach, mustard greens, lollo rosso lettuce, *tomyo* pea sprouts, Swiss chard used here)

¼ cup (50ml) Spicy Lemon Dressing (page 172)

METHOD

1. Have ready a large saucepan of boiling water (enough to cover the lobster) and a bowl of iced water. Add a pinch of sea salt to the boiling water and scald the lobster over high heat for 4 minutes. Plunge the lobster into the iced water, then remove the meat from the shell. Cut into bite-size pieces.

2. Bring about 1 inch (2.5cm) of oil in a small saucepan to 320°F (160°C). Deep-fry the garlic slices until crisp.

3. Lightly grill the mushroom caps.

4. Arrange the salad greens, mushrooms and lobster on a serving dish. Pour the Spicy Lemon Dressing over all and decorate with the garlic chips.

SPICY LEMON DRESSING TASTES GREAT with piping-hot tempura.

CRISP SALMON SKIN IS FAN-TASTIC IN COMBINATION WITH SALAD GREENS AND A ZESTY Jalapeño Dressing.

"WHEN I WAS A CHILD, WE USED TO EAT GRILLED SALTED SALMON AND RICE FOR BREAKFAST, and my favorite bit was always the skin on the salmon. Smoked salmon is a familiar item on sushi menus in the U.S. but the skin is often discarded. I save the skin, grill it until crisp and serve it as a popular sushi roll (Salmon Skin Roll, page 163)."

THE KEYNOTE OF THE DRESSING COMES FROM THE TARTNESS OF LEMON, A GREAT MATCH WITH THE SWEETNESS OF CRUSTACEANS LIKE SHRIMP AND CRAB. GARLIC CHIPS ADD A SAVORY ROASTED NOTE.

SEASONAL MUSHROOMS
ARE SAUTÉED IN
BUTTER, TOSSED WITH
A FRAGRANT *YUZU*
DRESSING AND SERVED ON
A BED OF LETTUCE.

THIS SALAD COMBINES TWO
OF MY FAVORITE
INGREDIENTS, WATERCRESS
AND BLACK SESAME. USING
THE WATERCRESS STALKS
IN THE DRESSING INTENSIFIES
THE WATERCRESS BOUQUET.

MUSHROOM SALAD WITH YUZU DRESSING

INGREDIENTS ———————————— serves 4

4 ounces (120g) assorted mushrooms, cut into uniform bite-size pieces (*shiitake, enoki, shimeji, maitake,* pleurote du panicaut, white mushrooms, trumpet mushrooms, girolles and *yanagi matsutake* used here)

4 teaspoons clarified butter

5 tablespoons plus 1 teaspoon Yuzu Dressing (page 173)

2 ounces (60g) lollo rosso lettuce

asatsuki chives, cut into 1 1/2-inch (4-cm) lengths

yuzu citrus rind, thinly julienned

METHOD

1. *Maitake* and *yanagi matsutake* fall apart easily, so immerse these in boiling water for 15 to 20 seconds, then drain.

2. Put the clarified butter in a small heated frying pan. Add all the mushrooms except the *enoki, maitake* and *yanagi matsutake* and sauté over high heat. Combine all the mushrooms with the Yuzu Dressing in a mixing bowl.

3. Line a serving dish with the lettuce. Transfer the mushroom mixture to the dish and top with the *asatsuki* chives and *yuzu* strips.

BE CAREFUL NOT TO overcook the mushrooms.

WATERCRESS AND BLACK SESAME SALAD WITH WATERCRESS DRESSING

INGREDIENTS ———————————— serves 4

5 1/4 ounces (150g) watercress

2 tablespoons black sesame seeds, toasted

1/4 cup (50ml) Watercress Dressing (page 173)

20 *udo* curls (page 174)

7 carrot curls (page 174)

METHOD

1. Rinse and drain the watercress. Cut off the thick stalks and stir them into the dressing.

2. Toss the watercress and toasted black sesame seeds together with the Watercress Dressing in a mixing bowl.

3. Transfer the salad to a serving dish and top with *udo* and carrot curls.

BE GENEROUS WITH the sesame seeds!

EGGPLANT SPECIAL

MISO AND OIL ARE GOOD COMPANIONS TO EGGPLANT. DEEP-FRIED EGGPLANT
HALVES ARE PLUMPED UP WITH A TOPPING OF CHOPPED SHRIMP AND
SCALLOPS.

INGREDIENTS ———————————————————— serves 4

7 ounces (200g) fresh *kuruma*
  shrimp

7 ounces (200g) scallops

sea salt

vegetable oil for deep-frying

4 eggplants (aubergines)

4 sweet long green peppers

8 tablespoons Nobu-style Saikyo
  Miso (page 172)

4 tablespoons Creamy Spicy
  Sauce (page 170)

METHOD

1. Twist off the heads from the shrimp, then shell and devein
   them. Rinse briefly and drain. Rinse the scallops and drain.

2. Finely chop the shrimp and scallops. Mix them together with
   a little sea salt.

3. Preheat a grill or broiler. Bring about 3 inches (8cm) of oil in
   a medium saucepan to 355°F (180°C). Halve the eggplants
   lengthwise without removing the stalk caps and deep-fry
   for 2 to 3 minutes, without letting them go floppy. Halve the
   peppers lengthwise, sauté and sprinkle with a little sea salt.

4. Place the eggplants, cut side up, on the grill or the broiler
   pan. Spoon the shrimp and scallop mixture over them and cook
   for 3 to 4 minutes. Remove from the grill or broiler and spread
   a layer of Nobu-style Saikyo Miso and then a layer of Creamy
   Spicy Sauce on top of the eggplant. Return to the grill or
   broiler until the surface mixture turns golden brown.

5. Transfer the eggplants to individual plates with the pepper halves.

THE BEST WAY TO EAT THIS IS TO SPOON UP the eggplant and topping in each bite.

ASPARAGUS AND SALMON ROE WITH EGG SAUCE

THE BRIGHT GREEN OF THE FRIED ASPARAGUS WITH THE YELLOW EGG SAUCE AND THE ORANGE SALMON ROE TOPPING MAKES A COLORFUL DISPLAY.

INGREDIENTS ———————— serves 4

vegetable oil for deep-frying

12 green asparagus spears, about
   6 inches (15 cm) long

sea salt

Egg Sauce (use 4 egg yolks: page 170)

2 tablespoons salmon roe

METHOD

1. Bring about 3 inches (8 cm) of oil in a
   medium saucepan to 340°F (170°C).
   Deep-fry the asparagus spears for 1 to
   2 minutes, drain and sprinkle with a
   little sea salt. Cut the spears in half.

2. Line a serving dish with the Egg Sauce.
   Arrange the asparagus in it in 2 or 3
   layers. Spoon the salmon roe on top.

THE COLOR OF THE ASPARAGUS
is a vital element in this dish, so don't
overcook it.

151

TOMATO CEVICHE, NOBU STYLE

For this dish, I use SWEET JAPANESE FRUIT TOMATOES. The SHARPNESS of Ceviche Sauce is the perfect foil for them.

INGREDIENTS ——————— serves 4

¼ red onion, thinly sliced

2 fruit tomatoes, quartered

4 yellow cherry tomatoes, halved

4 teaspoons finely chopped cilantro (coriander) leaves

¼ cup (50ml) Ceviche Sauce (page 170)

cilantro sprigs for garnish

METHOD

Combine all the vegetables and cilantro together in a mixing bowl and toss gently with Ceviche Sauce. Transfer to a serving dish and top with a cilantro sprig.

TRY ADDING AVOCADO CUBES as a variation.

"FRUIT TOMATOES ARE SPECIALLY CULTIVATED ON THE ISLAND OF SHIKOKU. Since the amount of water given to them is restricted, their sugar content is as high as any fruit, but the yield is minimal. Tiny yet surprisingly sweet, these expensive tomatoes have only been available in Japan for about ten years and are not yet exported to the United States or Europe. Other regions in Japan produce similarly sweet tomatoes called 'sugar tomatoes' or 'perfect tomatoes.'"

SEMI-DRIED TOMATOES

FRUIT TOMATOES ARE DRIED SLOWLY FOR A REALLY CONCENTRATED TASTE. THEIR SWEET TARTNESS IS SUPERB.

METHOD

1. Preheat the oven to 212°F (100°C, gas ¼). Peel the fruit tomatoes by cutting a shallow X in the bottom and slipping them into a pot of boiling water for a few seconds. This loosens the skin so that it slips off easily. Keep the stem caps attached, if possible. Bake on a cookie sheet for 3 hours.

2. Remove from the cookie sheet and dry for around 6 hours in a well-ventilated place. Store in a refrigerator until ready to use.

SOBA-SOBA-SOBA RISOTTO

THIS DISH IS A MEDLEY OF *SOBA* RISOTTO, *SOBA* NOODLES AND *SOBA* SPROUTS.

INGREDIENTS ———————————— serves 4

Risotto

4 ounces (120g) buckwheat groats (*soba* seeds)

2 cups (400ml) Dashi (page 174)

1 ³/₄ ounces (50g) *enoki* mushrooms

1 ³/₄ ounces (50g) *shimeji* mushrooms

¹/₂ teaspoon sea salt

freshly ground black pepper

1 tablespoon light soy sauce

3 tablespoons arrowroot starch, dissolved in 6 tablespoons of water

• • •

5 ¹/₂ ounces (160g) *soba* noodles (page 89, omitting the squid ink)

1 ¹/₂ ounces (40g) *soba* sprouts

truffle oil

METHOD

1. Have ready a medium saucepan of boiling water and a bowl of iced water. Boil the groats for 10 minutes. Drain the groats in a sieve or colander and plunge into the iced water. Drain.

2. Make the risotto: Bring the *dashi,* groats and mushrooms to a boil in a medium saucepan over high heat. Turn the heat to low and cook for 1 to 2 minutes more. Add the sea salt, black pepper and soy sauce. Then add the arrowroot solution to the risotto to thicken. Turn off the heat.

3. Transfer the risotto to individual serving dishes and top with the noodles and sprouts. Drizzle with a few drops of truffle oil.

ENJOY the taste of *soba* at all stages of its life cycle.

SOBA RISOTTO WITH BLOWFISH

BLOWFISH IS CONSIDERED A WINTER LUXURY IN JAPAN.

INGREDIENTS ———————————— serves 4

4 ounces (120g) blowfish milt

2 tablespoons plus 2 teaspoons light soy sauce

6 ¹/₂ ounces (180g) blowfish fillets

Risotto

4 ounces (120g) buckwheat groats, boiled as in step 1 of Soba-Soba-Soba Risotto, above

2 cups (400ml) Dashi (page 174)

1 ³/₄ ounces (50g) *enoki* mushrooms

1 ³/₄ ounces (50g) *shimeji* mushrooms

¹/₂ teaspoon sea salt

freshly ground black pepper

1 tablespoon soy sauce

3 tablespoons arrowroot starch, dissolved in 6 tablespoons of water

• • •

4 teaspoons *asatsuki* chives, cut into fine rounds

truffle oil

METHOD

1. Preheat a grill or broiler. Steep the blowfish milt in the soy sauce for 5 to 10 minutes. Sear the milt. Cut the blowfish fillets into paper-thin slices using the *usu-zukuri* technique (page 19).

2. Make the risotto (step 2, Soba-Soba-Soba Risotto, above).

3. Transfer the risotto to individual serving dishes and top with the blowfish slices and milt. The heat of the dish will cook the fish slightly. Add a sprinkling of *asatsuki* chives and a few drops of truffle oil.

BLOWFISH OR *FUGU* CONTAINS POISON in its liver and ovaries, so you might want to use another white fish instead.

SUSHI

Surprisingly, perhaps, after so many years as a sushi chef, I still adore sushi. Even when working I can rarely resist the temptation of fixing myself a sushi snack if I notice an especially good topping ingredient.

All sushi comes in standard shapes and sizes, so you might think the flavors don't vary that much either. Yet all grades of tuna from *o-toro* to red meat tuna, all white fish from sea bream to flounder, and all shellfish from ark shell to cockle shell have distinct flavors. The secret to good sushi is the harmony between quality topping and the tastiness of the vinegared rice. And though I experiment with different sauces and flavors in my other dishes, there is nothing better with sushi than plain old soy sauce. Working in the U.S., I discovered that people don't seem to like *hikarimono* ("shiny" fish, such as mackerel) as much as the Japanese do. But this may be because sushi chefs there simply don't offer shiny fish toppings, either because they assume people won't like them, or because the chefs themselves don't like them. I love *hikarimono*, and by serving these fish, I allow my sushi diners to get to know and enjoy a greater variety of sushi. Speaking of variety,

I've recently expanded my sushi repertoire to include such diverse ingredients as foie gras, Kobe beef, grilled *toro*, codfish milt in winter and also shark's fin and caviar. I even made moose sushi in Alaska once when I was given the meat by a hunter!

Having said that, I believe sushi is best when made with seafood, although there are no hard-and-fast rules—think of the hand-rolled sushi parties held these days featuring cheese or sausage. I hope this book encourages you to buy toppings that you want to eat, and to learn how to make good sushi rice. You can toast your own *nori* sheets over the gas burner at home to make it crisp and deepen its flavor. I used to toast a lot of *nori* this way when I was an apprentice sushi chef in Tokyo.

Finally—and I don't want to press the point—there is a certain way to eat sushi. You should dip the topping—not the rice—in the soy sauce, and only sparingly. *Wasabi* is already included in the sushi so you don't need extra in the soy sauce. And toppings brushed with *tsume* sauce do not require any soy sauce. The same goes for the omelette, which is already sufficiently seasoned.

VINEGARED SUSHI RICE

INGREDIENTS ——————————————— makes 14 ¾ cups (1.85kg)

Sushi rice (called *shari*) makes 14 cups (1.75kg)

4 ½ cups (720g) short-grain rice

4 ½ cups (900ml) water

Sushi rice vinegar (called *shari-zu*) makes 1½ cups (300ml)

1 cup (200ml) red vinegar

2 tablespoons plus 2 teaspoons sea salt

1 tablespoon *mirin*

10 tablespoons plus 1 teaspoon granulated sugar

1 ½-inch- (4-cm-) square sheet *konbu*

METHOD

1. Cook the rice: Rinse and rub the rice in repeated changes of cold water until the water turns from cloudy to clear. Drain in a sieve. Add the water to the rice in a heavy, large saucepan and bring to a boil over high heat. Boil for 1 minute. Turn the heat down to low and cook for 5 minutes. Finally, turn the heat up to high for 10 seconds. Remove from the heat and let the rice sit for 15 minutes. Alternatively use an automatic rice cooker.

2. Make the sushi rice vinegar: Simmer ¾ cup (150ml) of vinegar, sea salt, *mirin* and sugar in a small saucepan over medium heat to dissolve the sugar. Do not allow it to boil. Add the *konbu* and remove from heat. When cool, add the remaining vinegar because heating tends to destroy its bouquet. This will yield 1½ cups (300ml) of sushi rice vinegar, which is the minimum possible yield. In this recipe only ¾ cup (150ml) is used. The basic rice-to-vinegar ratio is 6:1 or 1 cup of vinegar for every 6 cups of uncooked rice.

3. Transfer the freshly cooked rice to a wooden Japanese rice tub or a similarly wide and shallow container. Pour ¾ cup (150ml) of the vinegar mixture all over the rice. While the rice is still hot, mix quickly with a rice paddle or flat wooden spoon, using a slicing motion. Leave to cool. Use the rice before it becomes too hard.

   The amount of water used to cook the rice will vary slightly according to the season. Less water should be used with newly harvested rice.

RED VINEGAR IS MADE WITH SAKÉ LEES and is the preferred choice of sushi chefs because of its sweetness. Substitute regular rice vinegar where necessary.

SOFT SHELL CRAB ROLL, HOUSE ROLL, SALMON SKIN ROLL

My three popular rolls are based on the traditional Japanese *futomaki*—a thick roll cut into slices and typically containing egg, dried gourd shavings, cooked sea eel, mashed cooked fish and cucumber rather than raw ingredients. These rolls should be rolled firmly to prevent the fillings from falling out. All three contain avocado, which I use not only as a symbol of California where my work is based, but because I adore its rich taste, its texture and its green color.

SOFT SHELL CRAB ROLL

I ONLY SERVED SOFT SHELL CRAB DEEP-FRIED AS AN APPETIZER UNTIL A CUSTOMER ASKED ME TO ROLL IT SUSHI-STYLE WITH *NORI* AND RICE. LATER, I ADDED FLYING FISH ROE AND AVOCADO, AND WRAPPED IT ALL IN A SINGLE *DAIKON* PEEL.

INGREDIENTS ──────────────────────── makes 6 pieces

1 cup (130g) vinegared rice (page 158)

1 sheet dried *nori*, 4 inches (10 cm) x 7 ½ inches (19 cm), toasted

grated *wasabi* to taste

1 tablespoon *asatsuki* chives, chopped into fine rounds

1 tablespoon flying fish roe

1/12 avocado

vegetable oil for deep-frying

1 soft shell crab, about 2 ½ ounces (70g)

potato flour

1 straight and uniform *daikon*, with ends trimmed, peeled

METHOD

1. **Spreading the rice**

Spread the vinegared rice on the sheet of *nori*. Using your left hand to make sure the rice doesn't spill over the left side of the *nori* sheet, spread the rice out evenly toward the left by pressing—but not squashing—the rice with the fingertips of your right hand. Repeat, starting from the left (i.e. with your right hand stationary on the right side). You should make the rice a little thicker at each end of the *nori* in order to form a "bank." Leave about ⅜ inch (1 cm) of the *nori* sheet free of rice at the side furthest from you.

1

2. **Adding the *wasabi* and filling**

When the rice is thoroughly and evenly spread over the *nori*, apply an unbroken streak of *wasabi* across the middle with one finger. Then, using a spoon, spread the *asatsuki* chives and the flying fish roe evenly over the *wasabi* and across the rice. Add the avocado on top.

3. Bring about 3 inches (8 cm) of oil in a small saucepan to 355°F (180°C). Dust the soft shell crab with potato flour and deep-fry for 3 to 4 minutes. Drain. Cut the crab in half and add it to the roll while the crab is still hot. Because the crab is the bulky part of the filling it should be firmly compressed before rolling. This will make rolling easier.

2

4. **Rolling with *nori***

Lift the end of the *nori* nearest you and carefully roll it over the filling, pressing down as you go.

5. **Making the *daikon* peel**

Holding an 8-inch (20-cm) knife firmly, move the *daikon* against the knife, turning the *daikon* gradually to cut the flesh into a paper-thin ribbon. This is called *katsura-muki*. You should end up with a strip 4 inches (10 cm) by 12 inches (30 cm).

6. **Rolling with the *daikon* peel**

Place the *nori* on top of the strip of *daikon* and roll away from you.

7. **Cutting**

Press down on the roll again at both ends to settle the filling, and trim the ends with a knife to tidy the shape. Starting from the middle, cut the roll into 6 pieces of equal size.

3

5

4

6

CENTERED ON FRIED SOFT SHELL CRAB, this roll allows you to enjoy a variety of textures and flavors in one mouthful, from the delicate crunch of flying fish roe to the rich creaminess of avocado. It's very popular at all my restaurants.

In my restaurants outside Japan, we use a paper-thin sheet of cucumber instead of *daikon*.

"MY FIRST TASTE OF SOFT SHELL CRAB WAS ABOUT TWENTY YEARS AGO IN AN ITALIAN RESTAURANT in Los Angeles. In Japan, many kinds of crab are eaten, but none just after they have shed their shells, so this was an entirely new taste for me. It seemed strange to me, as a sushi chef, that I hadn't known about this delicacy earlier."

7

HOUSE SPECIAL ROLL

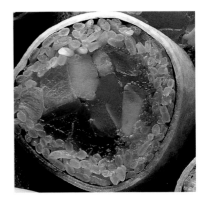

FILLED WITH ONLY FRESH INGREDIENTS, SUCH AS RAW TUNA, CRAB, FLYING FISH ROE AND AVOCADO, EACH HAS A DISCERNIBLE TASTE AND TEXTURE, RANGING FROM THE MILDNESS OF CRAB TO THE SPRINGINESS OF FLYING FISH ROE.

INGREDIENTS ─────────────────────────────────── makes 6 pieces

1 cup (130g) vinegared rice (page 158)

1 sheet dried *nori*, 4 inches (10 cm) x 7 1/2 inches (19 cm), toasted

grated *wasabi* to taste

1 tablespoon *asatsuki* chives, chopped into fine rounds

1 tablespoon flying fish roe

1/12 avocado

1/2 ounce (15g) fresh tuna

1/2 ounce (15g) smoked salmon

1/2 ounce (15g) white fish

1/2 ounce (15g) *hamachi*

1/3 ounce (10g) snow crab (meat from the leg)

1 straight and uniform *daikon*, with ends trimmed, peeled

METHOD

1. Spread the rice over the *nori*, spread the *wasabi* on the rice and add the *asatsuki* chives, flying fish roe and avocado as for the Soft Shell Crab Roll (page 160, steps 1 and 2).

2. Cut the fish into thin 1/2-inch- (1-cm-) thick, 4-inch- (10-cm-) long strips to fill the width of the *nori*. Cut the crabmeat into similar strips. Place the fish and crab strips across the roll. Roll and cut as for the Soft Shell Crab Roll (page 160, steps 4 to 7).

LOTS OF FRESH FISH IS ROLLED TOGETHER in this recipe. Enjoy the mellow smoothness and distinct flavors of each ingredient.

SALMON SKIN ROLL

SMOKED SALMON SKIN HAS ALWAYS BEEN A FEATURE IN MY SUSHI ROLLS. ENJOY THE BALANCE OF FLAVOR AND TEXTURE BETWEEN THE CRISPY SALMON SKIN, CREAMY AVOCADO AND SALTY, CRUNCHY PICKLED *YAMAGOBO* ROOT.

INGREDIENTS ———————————————————————— makes 6 pieces

1 cup (130g) vinegared rice (page 158)

1 sheet dried *nori*, 4 inches (10 cm) x 7 1/2 inches (19 cm), toasted

grated *wasabi* to taste

1 teaspoon toasted white sesame seeds

2 *shiso* leaves

1 tablespoon *asatsuki* chives, chopped into fine rounds

1/12 avocado

2 sticks pickled *yamagobo* root, cut the same length as the width of the *nori* sheet

1/2 tablespoon *kaiware daikon*, cut in half

1 1/2 ounces (40g) grilled smoked-salmon skin, chopped into 3/8-inch (1-cm) pieces

finely shredded dried bonito flakes

1 straight and uniform *daikon*, with ends trimmed, peeled

METHOD

1. Spread the rice over the *nori* as for the Soft Shell Crab Roll (page 160, step 1).

2. When the rice is thoroughly and evenly spread, apply an unbroken streak of *wasabi* across the middle. Arrange the filling on top in the following order: white sesame seeds, *shiso* leaves, *asatsuki* chives, avocado, pickled *yamagobo* root, *kaiware daikon*, smoked salmon skin and bonito flakes.

3. Roll and cut as for the Soft Shell Crab Roll (page 160, steps 4 to 7).

THIS IS A SUSHI ROLL STARRING GOLDEN GRILLED SALMON SKIN, accented by the saltiness of pickled vegetable.

SEA EEL DRAGON ROLL AND SUSHI

THE ADDITION OF AVOCADO GIVES THIS A COLORFUL TWIST.

INGREDIENTS

Dragon Roll (makes 6 pieces)

½ sheet dried *nori*, 4 inches (10 cm) x 7 ½ inches (19 cm), toasted

¾ cup (100g) vinegared rice (page 158)

1 teaspoon toasted white sesame seeds

grated *wasabi* to taste

1 ¾ ounces (50g) boiled sea eel (page 166), roughly chopped

1 tablespoon *asatsuki* chives, chopped into fine rounds

1 stick pickled *yamagobo* root, cut the same length as the width of the *nori* sheet

⅓ avocado, peeled and thinly sliced

Sea Eel Nigiri Sushi (makes 1 finger of *nigiri* sushi)

¾ cup (100g) vinegared rice (page 158)

grated *wasabi* to taste

boiled sea eel (page 166), cut into a 4-inch (10-cm) strip

Tsume Sweet Sauce (page 166)

a little *yuzu kosho* seasoning

sea salt

1 or 2 stalks *hajikami* (page 174) for garnish

METHOD

Dragon Roll

1. Cover a bamboo rolling mat (page 19) with plastic wrap, and over it lay the *nori*. Spread out the rice as for the Soft Shell Crab Roll (page 160, step 1) and sprinkle with the sesame seeds.

2. Flip the rice-spread sheet of *nori* over, on top of the bamboo mat, so that the *nori* faces upward. Spread a streak of *wasabi* across the width of the *nori*. Arrange the eel strips, *asatsuki* chives and *yamagobo* root over it. Roll using the bamboo mat. Remove the plastic wrap.

3. On another piece of plastic wrap, spread out the avocado slices to the same width as a *nori* sheet. Place the *nori*-and-rice roll of step 2 on the avocado and roll again with the bamboo mat.

4. Starting from the middle, cut into 6 pieces of equal size and remove the plastic wrap.

Sea Eel Nigiri Sushi

With one finger, press the rice into a firm oval in the palm of your other hand. Spread with grated *wasabi* to taste. Lay the eel on top of the rice and pinch together. Coat the eel served skin side up with Tsume Sweet Sauce. Sprinkle *yuzu kosho* seasoning and sea salt on the eel served flesh side up. Serve with *hajikami*.

BOILED SEA EEL WITH TSUME SWEET SAUCE

SEA EEL SUSHI IS EATEN WITH TSUME SWEET SAUCE, SALT, OR SOMETIMES TOPPED WITH GRATED YUZU AND LEMON PEEL. THE RECIPE FOR TSUME IS SOMETHING OF A TRADE SECRET WHICH VARIES FROM RESTAURANT TO RESTAURANT IN JAPAN.

INGREDIENTS

32 sea eels, about 9 pounds (4 kg)

8 quarts (8 l) water

18 ounces (500g) fine white sugar

1 ¼ cup (250ml) soy sauce

1 cup (200ml) saké

Sauce

9 ounces (250g) fine white sugar

1 ½ cups (300ml) soy sauce

METHOD

1. Filet the eels (page 136). Rinse them well in water to remove the sliminess from the skin. Drain.

2. In a large saucepan bring to a boil the water, sugar, soy sauce and saké and immediately add the eels. Cover with a lid dropped directly over the surface of the ingredients and simmer for 30 minutes, without boiling. Remove saucepan from heat and cool to touch.

3. Taking care not to break the eels, remove them from the boiling liquid and lay them out on a metal tray. They will firm up eventually as they cool to room temperature. These eels will be used as sushi toppings.

4. Make the sauce: Strain the liquid left after the eels have been removed. Add the sugar and soy sauce and reheat to a simmer over medium heat. Simmer until the liquid is thick enough to dribble in a sticky thread from a spoon. Remove from the heat.

THIS MAKES THE MINIMUM POSSIBLE YIELD for the Tsume Sweet Sauce. *Tsume* is also used with stewed clams, *shako* (mantis shrimp) and steamed abalone, as well as octopus and squid. If sushi comes with *tsume*, you don't need any soy sauce.

NOBU SAUCES AND BASICS

MUSTARD SU-MISO SAUCE

AJI PANCA SAUCE

CREAMY SPICY SAUCE

NOBU-STYLE SAIKYO MISO

JALAPEÑO SALSA

CEVICHE SAUCE

YUZU DRESSING

WASABI PEPPER SAUCE

MATSUHISA SALSA

MATSUHISA DRESSING

WATERCRESS DRESSING

MAUI ONION SALSA

EGG SAUCE

AJI AMARILLO SAUCE

AJI AMARILLO SAUCE

2 tablespoons plus 1 teaspoon *aji amarillo* paste
¼ cup (50ml) rice vinegar
1 tablespoon plus 1 teaspoon soy sauce
2 teaspoons lemon juice
2 teaspoons *yuzu* juice
2 tablespoons grapeseed oil

Combine all the ingredients.

YIELD: ¾ cup (150ml)

USED IN: Grilled Octopus with Miso Anticucho Sauce (page 78)

AJI PANCA SAUCE

½ teaspoon dried oregano
2 tablespoons plus 1 teaspoon *aji panca* paste
¼ cup (50ml) rice vinegar
1 teaspoon sea salt
1 teaspoon freshly ground black pepper
1 tablespoon finely grated garlic
1 ½ teaspoons powdered cumin
2 tablespoons saké
2 tablespoons grapeseed oil

1. Crush the oregano using a mortar and pestle to release its aroma.

2. Combine all the ingredients except the oil. When the salt is fully dissolved, add the oil.

YIELD: ¾ cup (150ml)

USED IN: Grilled Octopus with Miso Anticucho Sauce (page 78)

CEVICHE SAUCE

4 tablespoons lemon juice
2 teaspoons *yuzu* juice
½ teaspoon sea salt
1 teaspoon soy sauce
½ teaspoon finely grated garlic
½ teaspoon grated ginger
½ teaspoon freshly ground black pepper
1 teaspoon *aji amarillo* paste

Combine all the ingredients.

YIELD: 5 tablespoons plus 1 teaspoon

USED IN: Seafood Ceviche, Nobu Style (page 118) and Tomato Ceviche, Nobu Style (page 152)

CREAMY SPICY SAUCE

This is a simple homemade mayonnaise of egg yolk, oil and vinegar. Variations include the addition of spicy ingredients like mustard, *wasabi*, spicy cod roe, jalapeño, as well as soy sauce and *miso* paste. The most popular variation is this one with chili garlic sauce.

2 egg yolks
½ teaspoon sea salt
white pepper
2 teaspoons rice vinegar
1 cup (200ml) vegetable oil
1 tablespoon plus 1 teaspoon chili garlic sauce, passed through sieve

1. Make the mayonnaise by beating the egg yolks with a whisk in a bowl, adding the sea salt, a little white pepper and rice vinegar, and then gradually whipping in the vegetable oil a little at a time. Take care that the mayonnaise doesn't separate.

2. Stir in the chili garlic sauce.

YIELD: 1 cup (200ml)

USED IN: Scallops with Creamy Spicy Sauce (page 36), Matsuhisa Shrimp (page 48), Kuruma Shrimp Tempura with Creamy Spicy Sauce (page 52) and Eggplant Special (page 150)

EGG SAUCE

My egg sauce recipe was actually given to me by *Dynasty* star Linda Evans, a frequent diner at the restaurant I worked at before I opened Matsuhisa, when the show was at the peak of its popularity. One day after chatting about food, she came with me to the kitchen, where together we made her egg sauce.

4 egg yolks
2 tablespoons plus 1 teaspoon lemon juice
1 teaspoon soy sauce
2 tablespoons plus 1 teaspoon clarified butter (page 173)

1. Beat the egg yolks in a bowl. Add the lemon juice and the soy sauce and mix.

2. Add the clarified butter gradually so that it doesn't separate, mixing as you go.

YIELD: 3/4 cup (150ml)

USED IN: Abalone Shabu-shabu with Egg Sauce and Caviar (page 30), Spinach-Wrapped Sea Urchin with Egg Sauce (page 42) and Asparagus and Salmon Roe with Egg Sauce (page 151).

JALAPEÑO DRESSING

1 finely chopped jalapeño
4 tablespoons rice vinegar
1/2 teaspoon finely grated garlic
1 teaspoon sea salt
5 tablespoons grapeseed oil

Mix the jalapeño with the rice vinegar in a food processor. Add the other ingredients and mix again.

YIELD: 1/2 cup (100ml)

USED IN: Salmon Skin Salad with Jalapeño Dressing (page 146)

JALAPEÑO SALSA

2 finely chopped jalapeños
1 1/4 cups (125g) finely chopped onion
1 teaspoon sea salt
5 teaspoons extra virgin olive oil
5 tablespoons lemon juice

Combine all the ingredients.

YIELD: 1 3/4 cups (350ml)

USED IN: Oysters with Nobu's Three Salsas (page 38)

MATSUHISA DRESSING

This dressing was created to make sashimi more appealing and to satisfy my American customers' love of salad for lunch. Originally, I offered three salad dressings with soy sauce, shiso and ume as their respective bases, but the Matsuhisa Dressing with its soy sauce base proved the most enduring. Use Maui onions to maximize sweetness.

3/4 cup (70g) finely chopped onion
2 tablespoons plus 2 teaspoons soy sauce
1 tablespoon plus 1 teaspoon rice vinegar
2 teaspoons water
1/2 teaspoon granulated sugar
a pinch sea salt
1/4 teaspoon powdered mustard
a pinch freshly ground black pepper
4 teaspoons grapeseed oil
4 teaspoons sesame oil

Combine all the ingredients except the oils. When the salt is fully dissolved, add oils.

YIELD: 1 3/4 cups (350ml)

USED IN: Sashimi Salad with Matsuhisa Dressing (page 144)

MATSUHISA SALSA

1/2 cup (60g) finely chopped onion
1 tablespoon soy sauce
1/2 cup rice vinegar
1/2 teaspoon sea salt
1/4 teaspoon chili garlic sauce
1/4 teaspoon chili oil
1/4 teaspoon finely grated ginger
1 tablespoon grapeseed oil
1/2 cup (10g) finely chopped parsley leaves

Combine all the ingredients. Add the parsley just before use.

YIELD: 1 1/2 cups plus 2 tablespoons (330ml)

USED IN: Oysters with Nobu's Three Salsas (page 38)

MAUI ONION SALSA

1 cup (100g) finely chopped Maui onion
3/4 cup (105g) finely chopped tomato
6 tablespoons Ponzu (page 174)
2 teaspoons orange juice (freshly squeezed)
1 teaspoon hot chili sauce

Combine all the ingredients.

YIELD: 2 1/4 cups (450ml)

USED IN: Oysters with Nobu's Three Salsas (page 38) and Aori Squid with Maui Onion Salsa (page 81)

Matsuhisa Dressing is bottled and sold as Onion Soy Sauce Dressing

MUSTARD SU-MISO SAUCE

1 teaspoon powdered Japanese mustard
2 teaspoons hot water (104°F/40°C)
8 tablespoons (150g) Nobu-style Saikyo Miso (below)
2 tablespoons plus 1 teaspoon rice vinegar

1. Dissolve the mustard powder in a bowl with the hot water and blend into a thick paste.

2. Add the *miso* and rice vinegar. Mix well.

YIELD: ¾ cup plus 1 tablespoon plus 1 teaspoon (170ml)

USED IN: Steamed Abalone with Mustard Su-miso Sauce and Junsai (page 28), Monkfish Pâté with Caviar and Mustard Su-miso Sauce (page 98) and Toro Steak with Wakame Mustard Su-miso Sauce (page 134)

NOBU-STYLE SAIKYO MISO

¾ cup (150ml) saké
¾ cup (150ml) *mirin*
2 cups (450g) white *miso* paste
1 ¼ cups (225g) granulated sugar

1. Bring the saké and *mirin* to a boil in a medium saucepan over high heat. Boil for 20 seconds to evaporate the alcohol.

2. Turn the heat down to low and add the *miso* paste, mixing with a wooden spoon. When the *miso* has dissolved completely, turn the heat up to high again and add the sugar, stirring constantly with the wooden spoon to ensure that the bottom of the pan doesn't burn. Remove from heat once the sugar is fully dissolved. Cool to room temperature.

YIELD: 3 cups (800g)

USED IN: Grilled Octopus with Miso Anticucho Sauce (page 78), Fairy Squid with Kinome Sumiso Sauce (page 90), Black Cod with Miso (page 124) and Eggplant Special (page 150)

SAKÉ SOY SAUCE

¾ cup (150ml) Nikiri Zaké (page 174)
5 tablespoons soy sauce

Combine all the ingredients.

YIELD: 1 cup plus 1 tablespoon plus 2 teaspoons (225ml)

USED IN: Squid Pasta with Light Garlic Sauce (page 82)

SPICY LEMON DRESSING

I created this dressing in response to a request from a Los Angeles grocer to come up with a recipe using their packets of mixed mushrooms, which were then sold with the recipe for the resulting Spicy Lemon Dressing printed on the packet.

¼ cup (50ml) lemon juice
1 tablespoon plus 2 teaspoons soy sauce
½ teaspoon finely grated garlic
¼ teaspoon chili garlic sauce, passed through sieve
½ teaspoon sea salt
a little freshly ground black pepper
4 tablespoons plus 2 teaspoons grapeseed oil

Combine all the ingredients except the oil. When the salt is fully dissolved, add oil.

YIELD: ¾ cup (150ml)

USED IN: Lobster Salad with Spicy Lemon Dressing (page 146)

SPICY LEMON GARLIC SAUCE

1 cup (200ml) Nikiri Zaké (page 174)
2 tablespoons plus 2 teaspoons soy sauce
1 teaspoon chili garlic sauce, passed through sieve
1 teaspoon grated garlic
2 tablespoons plus ½ teaspoon lemon juice
1 tablespoon plus ½ teaspoon *yuzu* juice
¼ teaspoon finely grated ginger
1 tablespoon plus ½ teaspoon grapeseed oil

Combine all the ingredients.

YIELD: 1 ½ cups (300ml)

USED IN: Scampi with Spicy Lemon Garlic Sauce (page 50)

SPICY SOUR SAUCE

1 cup (200ml) lemon juice
2 teaspoons chili garlic sauce, passed through sieve
scant tablespoon light soy sauce
scant tablespoon soy sauce

Combine all the ingredients.

YIELD: 1 cup plus 2 tablespoons plus 1 teaspoon (235ml)

USED IN: Spicy Sour Botan Shrimp (page 54)

TABBOULEH SALSA

5 ¼ ounces (150g) cucumber
5 ¼ ounces (150g) tomato
5 ¼ ounces (150g) red onion
½ teaspoon sea salt
¼ teaspoon freshly ground black pepper
1 teaspoon finely chopped garlic
½ teaspoon *aji panca* paste
1 teaspoon lemon juice
1 teaspoon *yuzu* juice
1 teaspoon extra virgin olive oil
1 cup finely chopped parsley leaves

1. Dice the cucumber, tomato and red onion into ¼-inch (5-mm) cubes.

2. Combine the vegetable mixture with all the other ingredients in a small bowl.

YIELD: 4 cups (800ml)

USED IN: Grilled Scallops with Tabbouleh Salsa (page 34)

TOSA-ZU

5 tablespoons plus 1 teaspoon soy sauce
8 tablespoons rice vinegar
1/8 ounce (4g) dried bonito flakes

1. Heat the soy sauce and rice vinegar in a small saucepan over medium heat. Remove from heat as soon as the mixture begins to give off steam, and add the bonito flakes.

2. Cool to room temperature and strain out the bonito flakes.

YIELD: 1 cup (200ml)

USED IN: Baked Monkfish Medley with Tosa-zu (page 102)

WASABI PEPPER SAUCE

I came up with Wasabi Pepper Sauce when I discovered my customers liked *wasabi* and soy sauce in generous amounts with sushi and sashimi. First I blended a solution of powdered *wasabi* dissolved in water with soy sauce (fresh *wasabi* doesn't thicken), then I added a little butter and heated it. The result was quite unlike other soy sauce based mixtures; for a start it was syrupy, and the heating process had mellowed the nostril-burning sting of the *wasabi*. I added black pepper and served my first Wasabi Pepper Sauce simply with rice.

Wasabi Pepper Sauce was an instant hit, so I began serving it over fried fish, sautéed scallops and so on. Due to popular demand, I also began bottling it as my first commercially available sauce. I eventually stopped selling it as it doesn't keep very long, but Wasabi Pepper Sauce is still on the menu in more refined forms. I thin it with *dashi* if it's too strong and salty, or add a little saké and substitute butter for olive oil and ginger for garlic according to diners' requests. "The customer is a god," as we say in Japanese, and I'm happy to go along with that.

3 tablespoons powdered *wasabi*
2 tablespoons and 1 teaspoon water
2 tablespoons soy sauce
2 tablespoons low sodium soy sauce
8 tablespoons Dashi (page 174)

Dissolve the powdered *wasabi* in the water and combine with the other ingredients. Powdered *wasabi* tends to settle, so mix again before using.

YIELD: 1 cup (200ml)

USED IN: Abalone with Wasabi Pepper Sauce (page 26) and Toro Tartare with Caviar (page 132)

WATERCRESS DRESSING

I love watercress, which grows in summer in the creek on my regular Californian golf course. Watercress has a rather French image, but mixed with sesame seeds, the peppery flavor of its leaves turns into something different. The hard stalks are made into paste in a mixer and used as dressing in this watercress medley.

2 ounces (55g) watercress stalks, boiled lightly
2 teaspoons sea salt
1/2 tablespoon freshly ground black pepper
1/2 cup (100ml) rice vinegar
1/4 cup (50ml) grapeseed oil

Combine all the ingredients and mix in a blender.

YIELD: 1 cup (200ml)

USED IN: Watercress and Black Sesame Salad with Watercress Dressing (page 149)

YUZU DRESSING

These days, *yuzu* is used in Italian and even French cooking; but when I started making food containing *yuzu* it was unusual—and expensive—to do so. But I persevered, not only because it has a characteristic Japanese scent but because its taste is unlike lemon and its fragrance many times more potent. Once my customers came to appreciate the taste of *yuzu*, I made it the star of its own dressing. It's a shame I can't get hold of Peruvian lemons in the U.S., as their acidity is far stronger than any American variety. I use *yuzu* and lemons together instead.

1/4 cup (50ml) *yuzu* juice
5 teaspoons soy sauce
1/2 teaspoon freshly ground black pepper
1/2 teaspoon finely grated garlic
6 tablespoons grapeseed oil

Combine all the ingredients.

YIELD: 3/4 cup plus 1 tablespoon plus 1 teaspoon (170ml)

USED IN: Scallop Filo with Truffle Yuzu Sauce (page 32) and Mushroom Salad with Yuzu Dressing (page 149)

AMA-ZU (SWEET VINEGAR)

8 tablespoons rice vinegar
6 tablespoons granulated sugar
2 1/2 teaspoons sea salt

Heat the rice vinegar, sugar and sea salt in a small saucepan over medium heat until the sugar has fully dissolved. Remove from heat immediately. (Do not leave on heat longer, as the acidity of the rice vinegar will boil off.) Cool to room temperature.

YIELD: 1 cup plus 1 tablespoon plus 1 teaspoon (220ml)

CLARIFIED BUTTER

Butter contains milk solids that separate from the butterfat and burn. You can cook with butter at higher temperatures if you first remove these solids by clarifying the butter. Melt unsalted butter in a saucepan over low heat without stirring. When completely melted the butter will have separated into three layers. Skim off and discard the foamy layer of milk solids on top. The clear yellow butter beneath it is the clarified butter. Carefully pour it off into a container, leaving the milky liquid behind. Keep covered, refrigerated or frozen.

DASHI

Few non-Japanese appreciate the delicate flavor of *dashi* as much as Japanese do. I remember being offended when a French chef whom I cooked with at a charity event boasted that his French sauces took a week to make whereas my *dashi* was ready in ten minutes. So I told him about the long and labor-intensive process needed to produce the *konbu* and dried bonito flakes that are the essence of *dashi*. *Konbu* is cultivated for about two years before being carefully sun-dried. Well over six months are necessary to make the dried flakes from the bonito fish. The French chef kept quiet after that.

1/3 ounce (10g) piece of *konbu*
1 quart (1l) water
1 ounce (30g) dried bonito flakes

Heat the *konbu* and water slowly in a large saucepan over medium heat to bring out its full flavor. Just before the water boils, take out the *konbu* (to prevent scum forming), add the bonito flakes and turn off the heat. After the bonito flakes have sunk to the bottom of the pan, strain through a fine-mesh sieve lined with paper towels.

YIELD: 4 cups (800ml)

GARI (PICKLED GINGER)

This is best made with young ginger.

1. Wash the young ginger under cold water (but don't scrub) to remove any dirt. Do not peel. Use a slicer or a sharp knife to slice very thinly and immediately soak the slices in cold water. This prevents discoloration. Rinse again and drain.

2. Pickle overnight in *ama-zu* sweet vinegar (page 173).

If using regular ginger:

1. Peel the ginger and slice thinly. Pour hot water (double the amount of ginger) over the ginger. Stir lightly and sprinkle with sea salt (equal to 3% of the mass of the ginger). Let the ginger sit until the salt is absorbed completely. Rinse and squeeze out the water.

2. Pickle overnight in *ama-zu* sweet vinegar (page 173).

GINGER SPEARS

Peel the ginger, slice thinly and julienne as finely as possible. Plunge briefly in cold water and drain.

HAJIKAMI GINGER PICKLED IN SWEET VINEGAR

Remove any sand and debris and cut the ginger into 6-inch (15-cm) lengths. Briefly plunge the ginger into a pot of boiling water to which rice vinegar has been added (1 tablespoon per 1 quart/liter water). Drain and sprinkle thoroughly with sea salt. Let cool to room temperature. Leave for 12 hours to pickle in *ama-zu* which has been diluted 100% with water.

NIKIRI ZAKÉ (EVAPORATED SAKÉ)

Bring the saké to a boil in a saucepan and take off the heat as soon as its alcohol content has evaporated.

PONZU

4 tablespoons soy sauce
8 tablespoons rice vinegar
2 tablespoons lemon juice
3/4-inch- (2-cm-) square piece of *konbu*

Wipe the *konbu* clean with a cloth. Mix the remaining ingredients and add the *konbu*. Leave in the refrigerator overnight or longer.

YIELD: 1 cup plus 2 teaspoons (210ml)

SHREDDED DAIKON

Trim the ends of a peeled *daikon*. Using the *katsura-muki* technique (page 19), cut a thin, unbroken ribbon and julienne as finely as possible. Plunge briefly in cold water and drain.

TEMPURA BATTER

1 egg yolk
1 cup (200ml) iced water
1 cup (100g) all-purpose (plain) flour

Add the egg yolk to the iced water and mix well. Stir in the flour until just combined. The batter should not be smooth but a little lumpy. (Potato flour may be added for crispiness.)

UDO CURLS, CARROT CURLS

Peel the *udo* or carrot in a thin, unbroken strip 1 1/2 inches (4cm) wide. On a 45° angle, cut the *udo* or carrot into 1/2-inch- (1-cm-) wide strips. Wind the strips around a 1/2-inch- (1-cm-) diameter rod and place in iced water until required.

NER PLANS AND DESSERTS

...ses should be designed so that the customer finishes feel-
...and satisfied rather than uncomfortable and bloated. As a
...t my diners to eat and enjoy everything I put in front of
...when they say they are full it means simply that there was
...ood. I don't want my courses to
...gle to eat; I design them so that
...till has the capacity (literally) to
...st dish as much as the first. Too
...is never appreciated.

Dinner 1

Toro Tartare with Caviar (page 132)

New Style Sashimi (page 116)

Sashimi Salad with Matsuhisa Dressing (page 144)

Baby Squid Tempura with Squid Ink Sauce (page 84)

Chilean Sea Bass with Nobu's Black Bean Sauce
(page 106)

Sushi (page 156)

Bento Box (page 177)

Dinner 2

Matsuhisa Shrimp (page 48)

White Fish Tiradito, Nobu Style (page 120)

Mushroom Salad with Yuzu Dressing (page 149)

Kuruma Shrimp Tempura with Creamy Spicy Sauce
(page 52)

Black Cod with Miso (page 124)

Sushi (page 156)

Fruit Toban Yaki (page 180)

Dinner 3

Monkfish Pâté with Caviar and Mustard Su-miso Sauce
(page 98)

Seafood Ceviche, Nobu Style (page 118)

Lobster Salad with Spicy Lemon Dressing (page 146)

Sea Urchin Tempura (page 40)

Toro Toban Yaki (page 128)

Sushi (page 156)

Trio of Crèmes Brûlées (page 178)

Dinner 4

Oysters with Nobu's Three Salsas (page 38)

Toro with Jalapeño (page 130)

Watercress and Black Sesame Salad with Watercress
Dressing (page 148)

Frothing Blue Crab (page 64)

Freshwater Eel and Foie Gras (page 138)

Sushi (page 156)

Green Tea Parfait (page 179)

BENTO BOX

INGREDIENTS   serves 4

Chocolate soufflé

2 whole eggs plus 2 extra yolks

scant 3 ounces (88g) unsalted butter, plus more for greasing molds

scant 3 ounces (85g) sweetened chocolate (containing around 70% cocoa), finely chopped

¾ cup plus 2 tablespoons (100g) brown sugar

2 tablespoons plus ½ teaspoon cornstarch (cornflour)

confectioner's sugar (icing sugar)

Shiso syrup

1 large *shiso* leaf

4 tablespoons water

4 ½ tablespoons granulated sugar

scant tablespoon *mizuame*

Nobu-style Sesame Ice Cream or premium vanilla or green tea ice cream

fruit (any kind, cherries and starfruit here) for garnish

Sesame toffee

4 ½ tablespoons granulated sugar

1 tablespoon water

1 tablespoon white sesame seeds, toasted

1 tablespoon black sesame seeds, toasted

Sesame ice cream

9 tablespoons granulated sugar

4 egg yolks

4 tablespoons white sesame paste

1 cup (200ml) milk

1 cup (200ml) heavy (double) cream

METHOD FOR MAKING CHOCOLATE SOUFFLÉ MIXTURE

1. Beat together the whole eggs and the egg yolks and set aside at room temperature.

2. Melt the butter in a small saucepan over medium-low heat without burning, until just before the butter starts to froth. Set aside.

shiso syrup

3. Place the chocolate in a medium mixing bowl. Add the melted butter and whisk together until the chocolate melts. Next, add the brown sugar and cornstarch and mix. Finally, add the beaten eggs and mix quickly before straining the mixture through a sieve. The soufflé mixture should be left to sit covered in the refrigerator for a day before cooking.

METHOD FOR BAKING CHOCOLATE SOUFFLÉ

1. Preheat the oven to 355°–375°F (180°, gas 4, to 190°C, gas 5). Grease 4 oven-proof molds 3 inches (8cm) in diameter with melted butter.

2. Lay 4 pieces of parchment paper larger than the molds on a baking sheet and arrange the molds on top. Fill each with the soufflé mixture.

3. Bake for about 12 minutes. As soon as the soufflés are done, place them on individual plates and remove the parchment paper and molds. Do this quickly, otherwise the chocolate will harden. Sift confectioner's sugar through a sieve over the tops of the soufflés.

METHOD FOR SHISO SYRUP

Briefly dip the *shiso* leaf in boiling water, then plunge into iced water and pat dry with a paper towel. Chop the leaf finely. Bring the other ingredients to a boil in a small saucepan. Boil for 2 minutes over medium heat. When the syrup thickens slightly, add the finely chopped *shiso* leaf and let the syrup cool.

Raspberry sauce or any tart sauce is also a good match for the chocolate soufflé.

METHOD FOR NOBU-STYLE SESAME ICE CREAM

1. Make the toffee: Mix the sugar and water in a small saucepan and boil over medium heat until the syrup turns a light caramel color. Add the sesame seeds. Mix well with a wooden spatula. Spread the mixture out thinly on a baking sheet and leave to cool at room temperature. Once hard-

ened, break up the toffee into small pieces. Shake the pieces in a sieve to remove "dust."

2. Make the ice cream: Whisk together the sugar, egg yolks and white sesame paste in a medium bowl and set aside. Heat the milk in a small saucepan until it boils. Add the sugar-egg-sesame mixture and cook together over medium heat, scraping around the pan with a spatula to keep the bottom from burning. When the mixture has reached about 175°F (80°C), strain it quickly into a medium bowl and leave to cool. Mix in the fresh cream and complete by churning in an ice-cream maker. Just before the ice cream sets, add the sesame toffee pieces.

TO SERVE

For each serving, arrange a chocolate soufflé and a scoopful of sesame ice cream in a Japanese *jubako bento* box. Add the fruit and serve with the *shiso* syrup on the side. The syrup should be poured over the soufflé before eating. Make and serve the soufflé quickly before the chocolate hardens.

TRIO OF CRÈMES BRÛLÉES

serves 4

Basic brûlée ingredients

4 tablespoons heavy (double) cream
1 tablespoon plus 1 teaspoon milk
1 egg yolk
1 tablespoon plus ½ teaspoon granulated sugar
2 teaspoons fine brown sugar

Black sesame brûlée

1 teaspoon black sesame paste
1 teaspoon brandy

Ginger and truffle brûlée

1 ½ tablespoons fresh ginger, finely sliced without removing skin
1 teaspoon ginger wine
black truffle, finely sliced

Green tea brûlée

½ teaspoon green tea powder
1 teaspoon kirsch

kumazasa bamboo leaf for garnish, optional
fruit (strawberry, loquat and mint leaf here)

METHOD FOR MAKING THE BASIC BRÛLÉE

1. Heat the cream and milk in a small saucepan over medium heat until just before boiling. Whisk the egg yolk and sugar in a mixing bowl. Add the hot cream and milk mixture gradually, then mix again.

2. Preheat the oven to 335°–355°F (170°, gas 3, to 180°C, gas 4). Strain the mixture through a fine-mesh sieve to remove any small lumps. Discard any surface residue (white froth from the egg yolks) by blotting the surface with a paper towel or skimming with a spoon.

3. Pour the mixture into individual ramekins and bake standing in a pan of hot water reaching halfway up the sides of the ramekins for 20 to 25 minutes.

4. Cool to room temperature. Sprinkle fine brown sugar over the surface and scorch the surface lightly with a propane torch (blow torch) or place under the broiler (grill) to caramelize the sugar.

METHOD FOR BLACK SESAME BRÛLÉE

Follow as for basic brûlée, but add the black sesame paste at step 1 together with the egg yolks and sugar. Add the brandy after completing step 2.

METHOD FOR GINGER BRÛLÉE

Follow as for basic brûlée, but add the ginger together with the cream and milk at step 1. Add the ginger wine after completing step 2. Then add the truffle slices and mix.

METHOD FOR GREEN TEA BRÛLÉE

Follow as for basic brûlée, but add the green tea powder at step 1 together with the egg yolks and sugar. Add the kirsch after completing step 2.

TO SERVE

Lay a *kumazasa* bamboo leaf on a serving plate. Arrange the three different brûlées over it and garnish with the strawberry, loquat and mint leaf.

Putting the finished brûlée in the refrigerator will cause condensation to form on the caramelized surface.

GREEN TEA PARFAIT

Green tea parfait

1 teaspoon kirsch
9 tablespoons plus 1 teaspoon heavy (double) cream
2 tablespoons plus 2 teaspoons milk
1 tablespoon green tea powder
3 tablespoons granulated sugar
scant tablespoon (13ml) water
3 egg yolks

Azuki-espresso sauce

1½ tablespoons azuki beans
2 cups (400ml) water
½ cup plus 2 tablespoons (130ml) espresso
4½ tablespoons granulated sugar
1 teaspoon arrowroot starch, dissolved in 5 tablespoons plus 1 teaspoon water
1½ tablespoons large-pearl tapioca
aloe vera leaves

Choux decoration

scant cup (90g) all-purpose (plain) flour
pinch of salt
½ cup (90g) unsalted butter
6 tablespoons water
6 tablespoons milk
3 eggs, beaten
chervil for garnish, optional

METHOD FOR MAKING GREEN TEA PARFAIT

1. Add the kirsch to the cream and whip until soft peaks form. Set aside.

2. Heat the milk to about 175°F (80°C) in a small saucepan. Add the milk gradually to the green tea powder in a bowl. Mix the tea and the milk, taking care the tea doesn't form lumps. When thoroughly mixed, strain through a fine-mesh sieve and combine with the cream and kirsch mixture from step 1.

3. In a small saucepan, heat the sugar and water over medium heat to about 230°–240°F (110°–115°C). Remove from heat when the mixture starts to bubble. Do not stir the mixture.

4. In a separate bowl, mix the egg yolks with an electric mixer or hand-held whisk until the mixture becomes pale yellow. Gradually add the sugar syrup from step 3, beating until the mixture cools. When it has cooled to room temperature, add the

tea and milk mixture from step 2. Fold together gently with a rubber spatula, pour into parfait glasses and leave to set in the refrigerator.

METHOD FOR MAKING AZUKI-ESPRESSO SAUCE

1. Soak the azuki beans for about 10 hours in plenty of water. Change the water 2 or 3 times during the soaking process.

2. Drain the azuki beans and place in a small saucepan over high heat with plenty of water to cover. When it comes to a boil, pour off the liquid and add the measured 2 cups (400ml) of water. Simmer on a low heat. When the azuki beans are soft (after about 30 minutes), drain off all the liquid.

3. In a medium saucepan, bring the espresso, sugar and cooked azuki beans to a boil over medium heat. Boil for 4 to 5 minutes until well reduced.

4. Add the arrowroot solution and bring back to a boil. Remove from heat and leave to cool.

METHOD FOR PREPARING TAPIOCA

1. Place the tapioca beads in a small saucepan with plenty of hot water to cover and soak for an hour.

2. Bring the tapioca to a boil over medium heat. Simmer for 1½ to 2 hours until the beads are translucent and soft in the middle. Remove from the water and plunge briefly into iced water. Drain.

METHOD FOR PREPARING ALOE VERA LEAVES

Peel and discard the green skin from the leaves. Chop the peeled aloe into ½-inch (1-cm) chunks.

METHOD FOR MAKING CHOUX DECORATION

1. Mix together the flour and salt and set aside.

2. In a small saucepan, heat the butter, water and milk over medium heat. When the mixture comes to

a boil, add the flour and salt from step 1, mixing quickly with a wooden spatula so that it doesn't form lumps. Stir continuously to keep the bottom from burning, and cook for about 1 minute until the paste becomes glossy.

3. Quickly transfer the paste to a bowl. Add the beaten eggs and mix with a wooden spoon until smooth.

4. Preheat the oven to 320°F (160°C, gas 3). Transfer the paste to a pastry bag with a metal nozzle. Pipe the mixture onto a greased baking sheet in a lattice pattern.

5. Bake for about 15 minutes or until lightly browned. After the choux begins to color it also begins to burn easily, so take care.

TO SERVE

Take the green tea parfait out of the refrigerator about 10 minutes before serving. Pour the azuki-espresso sauce over the parfait and top with tapioca and aloe vera. Finish off by adding the choux decoration and chervil.

FRUIT TOBAN YAKI

INGREDIENTS   serves 4

Strawberry sauce

1 pound (500g) strawberries
3 tablespoons granulated sugar
2 teaspoons *mizuame*
2 thyme sprigs, about 4 inches (10 cm) long

• • •

1 banana
8 strawberries
½ papaya
20 blueberries
1 mango
¼ melon
8 grapes
unsalted butter
8 cherries

METHOD

1. Make the strawberry sauce: Remove the
   strawberry leaves and purée the fruit in a
   food processor. Transfer the purée to a
   medium saucepan and add the remaining
   sauce ingredients. Bring to a boil over
   medium-low heat. Simmer until reduced
   by half. Scrape the bottom of the saucepan
   with a wooden spatula while boiling so
   the mixture doesn't burn. Strain.

2. Cut the banana, papaya and mango into
   bite-size (but not too small) pieces. Peel
   the grapes and remove the seeds.

3. Preheat the oven to 355°F (180°C, gas 4).
   Grease a ceramic *toban* hotplate with
   butter and arrange the fruit on it. Bake for
   10 minutes. Be careful not to overcook or
   the fruit will soften and lose its "bite."

4. Remove the *toban* from the oven and
   immediately place over high heat until
   the fruit sizzles. Pour the sauce around
   the fruit. When the sauce starts to bubble, remove from heat and serve.

SAKÉ AND OTHER DRINKS

HOKUSETSU

Sado is the largest island in the Sea of Japan, twenty-two miles from the northern port of Niigata. The island is bisected by the same thirty-eighth parallel that separates the two Koreas. Famous for its cold, harsh winters, Sado was a place of criminal exile in the medieval period (mid-twelfth to sixteenth centuries). When gold and silver mines opened in 1601, the island prospered. Gold production has now dwindled and today rice, cuttlefish and yellowtail are its major products. Sado's many attractions include its scenic coast, historical sites and traditional songs and dances such as the Sado *okesa*. It is also home to the endangered *toki* or Japanese crested ibis. Hokusetsu—Nobu's preferred saké brewery—also reigns from the island of Sado.

Members of the Hazu family started as purveyors of saké and other alcoholic drinks in 1871 and have been producing their own highly original brews since 1886. The brewery adopted the name Hokusetsu, which means "Northern Snow," in 1993. A small, independent brewer with character and vision, Hokusetsu produces uncompromisingly dry sakés, many of which have been awarded Japan's most coveted prizes for brewing. While maintaining the highest standards of traditional saké brewing, the company has not been too timid to utilize state-of-the-art technology and develop creative

storage techniques, some inspired by tales from saké folklore.

Until Japan's first railways were built in the late nineteenth century, saké, like other products, was often transported by boat from the breweries on the Sea of Japan coast to drinkers in Edo (the old name for Tokyo) on the Pacific coast. Connoisseurs claimed that the saké that came across water always tasted better, that it was made smooth and mellow by the undulating motion of the ocean. With the aim of recreating this mellowness, Hokusetsu plays the music of the Japanese composer Kitaro to bottles of its renowned *Ongakushu* (literally "musical saké") for three years in a special cellar. Ultrasonic wave equipment is also used to this end. In 1987 Hokusetsu commissioned the world's first titanium containers to keep ultraviolet light from spoiling the saké.

Hokusetsu began exporting its products to the United States in 1990 and now sells its saké brews and beer exclusively through Nobu's restaurants throughout the world. Robert De Niro visited Sado and the brewery in 1998 when he came to Japan to launch the opening of Nobu Tokyo. A saké connoisseur, De Niro prefers to drink his favorite Hokusetsu tipples—the ten-year-old *Onigoroshi* and more recently the high-quality *Daiginjo YK35*—from a wooden cup, made from the Japanese cypress tree, together with a little salt sprinkled on one corner of the rim. For De Niro, Sado will always be fondly remembered as Saké Island.

MAKING SAKÉ

The basic ingredients of saké are rice and water. Most saké drunk in Japan today comes from huge modern factories that make use of stainless steel vats, biochemistry and computers. The basic brewing techniques, however, have changed very little since the 1500s when saké was first produced from polished white rice. Indeed, Hokusetsu, and many other small breweries, have not forgotten the old ways and make some brews, such as *Junmai Daiginjo*, almost entirely by hand. Saké is a living thing: Slight variations in taste depend on the quality of the rice, water and yeast, weather conditions at the time of brewing, the brewing temperatures used and

the skill of each worker involved. Ultimately, the success of the brewing process is decided by the experience and intuition of the master brewer or *toji*. Saké is brewed on the very coldest days of winter with rice harvested in the autumn. In April, the brewing process is complete and the new saké is tasted by the *toji* and the brewery owners.

Rice Polishing

Saké is made from polished rice. Brown rice is milled and the smaller white rice grains that remain are used for brewing. Brewers have known for a long time that the further rice is

polished, the finer the flavor of the saké. Generally the rice used in brewing is polished to 80% or less of its original size and to less than 40% for some top grades. Saké is most often classified by this rice-polishing ratio, and Hokusetsu's brews range from 68% to 35% for its two flagship brands, *Daiginjo KK35* and *Daiginjo YK35*.

Washing, Steeping and Steaming

Nuka or rice powder still clings to the surface of polished rice. This is removed by washing. Gentle hand-washing is required for top grades of saké which use delicate rice that has been polished to less than 50% of its original size. The rice is then soaked to allow the grains to absorb the desired amount of water. The more the rice has been polished the more quickly it absorbs water, so rice that has been polished to about 75% of its original size is usually left to soak overnight, while highly polished rice will only be steeped in water for a few minutes. Hokusetsu generally steeps its rice for about five minutes. The rice is then steamed to produce the all-important *koji* (saké mold) and to sterilize the rice. Hokusetsu steams its rice for sixty minutes at 216°F (103°C). The steamed rice is then divided and cooled depending on which of the stages of the brewing process it is to be used in.

Making *Koji* Rice

Koji is a mold (*Aspergillus oryzae*) which converts starch into sugar and also breaks down proteins. Some 20% of the steamed rice is cooled to about 86°F (30°C) and transferred to a special double-walled, sauna-like room that retains heat. Here, dried *koji* spores are scattered over the surface of the rice and kneaded in to distribute them evenly. After a few hours the rice is moved to shallow wooden trays which are placed on shelves and covered with a cloth. As the *koji* mold grows, the temperature of the rice rises. To ensure that the temperature of the rice does not get too high, workers stir it every four hours. After forty-eight hours, the boxes containing *koji* rice are removed from the warm *koji* room to stop the growth of the bacteria. The *koji* rice is then combined with steamed rice, water and yeast to make the basic mash or *moto*.

Making *Moromi* and Fermentation

The ingredients of the main mash or *moromi* (water, *koji* rice and steamed rice) are added to the starter mash in three stages over four days. This is called *san-dan jikomi*. Increasingly large amounts of these ingredients are added to the basic mash on the first, third and fourth days. No additions are made on the second day. This final mash is left to ferment for thirty days and results in the *moromi*, with a 17.5% alcohol content.

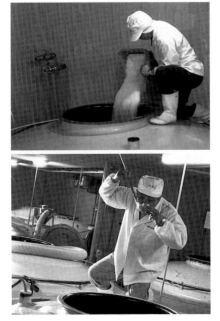

Pressing and Filtering

Almost all saké is now pressed in automatic pressing machines. A traditional *fune* press is also used for certain brews at some breweries. The *moromi* is poured into long bags (*saka-bukuro*) and stacked in the deep rectangular body of the press. For the first few hours, the saké trickles out under its own weight; later, a heavy lid is lowered and pressure slowly applied. On the following day, the bags are restacked and pressed once more. The fresh saké is called *shinshu* or "new saké." The caked lees that remain in the bags are called *saké kasu*, and are used in pickle-making and cooking.

Pasteurization, Storage and Dilution

The saké is pasteurized at 140°F (60°C) and then transferred to vats, where it is aged for about three months. Before bottling, the brewer will add water to dilute the saké to a level of between 15% and 17% alcohol and pasteurize it again.

Maturing

Some Hokusetsu brews—most notably *Honjozo Kinpakuri* and *Ongakushu*—are left to mature in a dark, cool cellar. Unique to Hokusetsu is the special treatment given to the bottles of saké in storage. *Onigoroshi* is kept at temperatures below 32°F (0°C). Saké freezes at 6°F (–15°C). Hokusetsu has also installed special ultrasonic wave equipment to mellow some of its brews, such as *Chojukushu*. A variation of this technique is used for its *Ongakushu*: Stereo equipment plays the New-Age music of a Japanese composer to this saké for three years.

HOW I CAME ACROSS HOKUSETSU

I first tasted Hokusetsu saké soon after Matsuhisa opened, when my friend, the Japanese rock musician Eikichi Yazawa, brought a bottle over. At the time Matsuhisa only served a sickly U.S.-made saké and I was amazed at how good the Hokusetsu tasted.

These days, most saké is made by allowing rice to ferment naturally without any additives, so the quality of the rice and the water determines the flavor. Saké used to be made with added alcohol and yeast, making it overly sweet and suitable only for serving hot. When I tasted the smoothness of chilled Hokusetsu saké, I decided I wanted it on my menu, especially as American attitudes toward saké were beginning to change. So I enlisted the aid of the trading firm that imported Japanese fish for me. We had to wait about a year to get permission to import. I rather sneakily asked the Hokusetsu brewery to limit exports of their top-ranked saké to me alone and they agreed.

Around that time, I was in Hawaii on business when some-body offered me a "special" saké that was unusually hard to come by. I recognized the taste and then the label as Hokusetsu. The same thing happened in Chicago, where I was again offered this saké to which I supposedly had the exclusive import rights. I was angry with the importers, even though I could understand why they wanted to sell as much of it as possible. Nevertheless I begged the brewery to hold off wider distribution, promising to pitch the saké myself.

Grateful for their trust, I took on more and more Hokusetsu brands, until all my restaurants in the U.S., Europe and even Japan stocked Hokusetsu products only, as will future branches. Thus, a little drink with a friend turned into a global enterprise. But more than the business profits, I believe that valuing the close ties forged in such a process brings its own kind of profit.

Now I've moved on from experimenting in ways of matching Hokusetsu sakés with my food to creating suitable saké cocktails myself.

WHITE PEACH SAKÉ

INGREDIENTS   serves 4

3 white peaches (large ripe ones)
2 ½ cups (500ml) water
¾ cup granulated sugar
½ Tahitian vanilla bean
1 cinnamon stick
¾ pint (390ml) saké (Hokusetsu *honjozo* grade)
2 teaspoons lemon juice

METHOD

1. Wash the peaches but do not peel. Cut them in half or in thirds.

2. In a large saucepan heat the water, sugar, vanilla bean and cinnamon stick over medium heat. When the mixture comes to a boil, add the peaches and their stones and simmer for about 3 minutes.

3. Remove the peaches, discard the stones and purée in a food processor. Strain the purée and the contents of the saucepan through a fine-mesh sieve.

4. Return the strained peach mixture to the saucepan over medium heat and boil until reduced to about one-third. Cool.

5. In a medium bowl combine the cooled peach mixture and the saké. Add lemon juice to taste.

6. Pour into a tall lipped jug or similar container with a spout and handle.

This drink can be made equally well with passion fruit, melon, cherries or berries.

MATSUHISA MARTINI

INGREDIENTS

saké (Hokusetsu *honjozo* grade)
vodka
sliced *gari* (page 174)
cucumber, thinly sliced for garnish

METHOD

Mix equal parts of saké and vodka with the *gari* in a shaker filled with ice, shake and pour into cocktail glasses. Garnish with cucumber.

NOBU-STYLE EGGNOG

INGREDIENTS   serves 1

1 tablespoon plus 1 teaspoon saké (Hokusetsu *honjozo* grade)
1 egg yolk, beaten
1 tablespoon plus 1 teaspoon Galliano
approx. 1 tablespoon plus 1 teaspoon sugar syrup
¾ cup (150ml) milk, heated but not boiled
hamabofu leaves for garnish, optional

METHOD

Heat the saké and combine with the egg yolk, Galliano and sugar syrup. Mix well and pour into a glass. Add the heated milk and mix well. Garnish with *hamabofu* leaves.

THE RESTAURANTS

At the time of going to press, I have eleven restaurants in nine cities in the United States, Europe and Japan, and more are planned for the future. Everything started, of course, with the opening of the Los Angeles Matsuhisa in 1987. Matsuhisa may not be as grand or as stylish as some of my other restaurants, but I like it just the way it is. It may not be as pretty as the rest, but I don't want to change anything. Los Angeles is my home and Matsuhisa is my base. It's the restaurant where I feel most at ease, happy and relaxed. After all, my wife Yoko and some other long-serving staff are all there. Many of my customers, who have also dined at the other restaurants, feel the same way about Matsuhisa, saying that going there helps them unwind too.

When we opened Matsuhisa, I wanted a very special glass case for the sushi toppings and had one custom-made by a friend who is an architect in Japan. He came all the way from Japan with three other friends to install it in time for the opening.

Many people have commented on the Nobu logo (which is also used throughout this book). In Tokyo, there used to be a basement supper bar in Shinjuku decorated with an impressive silhouette portrait by a famous Japanese artist. When I opened Matsuhisa, I looked at its bare white walls and remembered that silhouette. I wanted somebody to be in the restaurant at all times, so I asked an artist friend of mine to paint a life-size silhouette on the wall. The models, a range of people from construction workers and customers to friends and staff, stood against the wall as a bright light was beamed on them and the artist traced the outlines of their shadows. Each one looks exactly like the real person. In front of the sushi counter

is one of me preparing fish. This became the basis for the Nobu logo.

I'll always remember the time in 1999 when Roberto Benini won his Oscar for *Life Is Beautiful*. Before the Oscars, he and I had been discussing at Matsuhisa how many of my customers in movies, including actors like Robin Williams and Gwyneth Paltrow, had received Academy Awards. I joked that visitors to Matsuhisa always went away with Oscars. I was in Tokyo watching the Oscars ceremony on TV when it was announced that Benini had won Best Actor, and was moved when I saw him leap out of his chair in sheer delight. A few days later, he came to Nobu New York where he was greeted with a standing ovation from staff and customers.

David Rockwell, who designed the interior of my two New York restaurants as well as Nobu Las Vegas, always involved me in discussions about his general design concept. As I like my restaurants to have a warm, welcoming atmosphere, I asked him to use lots of wood. The kitchen was based on my own design, as it is in all my restaurants. Perhaps because it was my second restaurant and it was located in New York, my first and indeed lasting impression of David's design was that it was very fashionable. The star elements of the Nobu Next Door (opened in 1998) interior are the showcase display of Hokusetsu saké brews and the *nori*-papered wall.

After Nobu New York opened in 1994, I made a point of going out drinking with the staff after closing. One night after I got home, I realized that my wallet was missing. I assumed a colleague I'd been out with had picked it up, but when I called him, he said he hadn't seen it. I thought I'd lost it for good. A couple of days later, though, someone called the restaurant to say that they'd found my wallet. It had contained several thousand dollars, which I was sure I wouldn't see again. But I at least wanted my driver's license and credit cards back, so I took a cab to Brooklyn armed with champagne and caviar as a thank-you present. How delighted I was when I looked inside and saw that all the cash was still there! This isn't supposed to happen in New York! It was a miracle! In a magazine interview around that time, the only way I could express my feelings about this incident was to say, "I love New York!"

Only twice have I thought I was about to die. Once was when I was in a head-on collision on a freeway as a high-school student. The other was when Nobu New York was burgled.

One Sunday night after closing, I heard a staff member scream from the basement and the sound of gunfire as she was shot. The two robbers made their way to the first-floor kitchen, where they shot another staff member. I happened to be in the office behind the kitchen when this happened. I heard a third shot as a staff member was shot trying to escape.

The robbers then burst into the office looking for the safe. They put a gun to my back, demanding that I empty the safe. I calmly assumed I was about to die; but to tell the truth, I wasn't afraid—I just didn't know the combination. A colleague who was in the office with me did, however, and with trembling hands he opened it and handed the money over. They fled immediately. If he hadn't been there, maybe I would have been killed. Fortunately, this incident didn't claim any lives.

Keith Hobbs was responsible for designing Nobu London when it opened in 1997. I remember walking into the restaurant soon after the construction work was supposed to have been completed and staring at the plain, blank, white walls. "This can't be finished," I thought. "There must be some pictures or color coming." The staff had a good laugh when I expressed my puzzlement. Looking back on it now, of course, I can see how well it works—how very "London" it is.

I once made lunch for the late Princess Diana at Nobu London. I was struck by the firmness of her handshake when we first met, and her mentioning that she had read about me. I remember she drove a BMW; she came without a single bodyguard. I made her a light meal—vegetable tempura and lobster sashimi. I heard the sad news of her death sometime later in New York. Like the rest of the world, I was shocked. I will never forget her.

Matsuhisa Aspen (opened in 1998) used to be an old house with no commercial electricity or gas. The town of Aspen has legislation that prevents developers and owners from

modifying or damaging the external appearance of certain buildings, so we had to move the whole house intact in order to dig the basement, put in the electricty and gas and fix the plumbing. The main dining area at Matsuhisa Aspen is actually down in the basement, while the first floor can be reserved for private parties.

Nobu Tokyo (also opened in 1998) is my only restaurant that doesn't have a sushi bar. I knew my Tokyo customers would already have their own favorite sushi restaurants, and would be expecting something more from mine, so we ordered a humidor and had a room made into a cigar bar where customers could relax after a meal with a cigar. I asked the architect, Masami Komatsu, to include a staff shower—there's also one in Matsuhisa Aspen—and a recreation room. Personally, when designing a restaurant, I can't think of anything more

important than creating an environment in which the staff can work comfortably.

Jazz musician Kenny G was a regular at Matsuhisa. One day he invited me to a Los Angeles concert of his. I had only ever been to one concert before and wasn't really excited about music, but decided to go anyway and see what it was all about. I could tell from his performance, from the way he mingled with the audience, that he really loved his work and enjoyed entertaining fans. As he said to me afterward, he and I have pretty much the same attitude toward our chosen professions.

When I opened Nobu Malibu in 1999 I asked him to be a partner in the business. This was how Kenny G went from being a customer to a business associate—and, of course, a great friend.

MATSUHISA

Established January 1987—Beverly Hills

129 North La Cienega Blvd., Beverly Hills, CA 90211

Tel 310–659–9639   Fax 310–659–0492

MATSUHISA ASPEN

Established February 1998—Aspen

303 East Main St., Aspen CO 81611

Tel 970–544–6628   Fax 970–544–6630

NOBU NEW YORK

Established August 1994—Tribeca

105 Hudson in Tribeca, New York, NY 10013

Tel 212–219–0500   Fax 212–219–1441

NOBU NEXT DOOR

Established October 1998—Tribeca

105 Hudson in Tribeca, New York, NY 10013

Tel 212–334–4445   Fax 212–334–0044

NOBU LAS VEGAS

Established May 1999—THE HARD ROCK HOTEL & CASINO

4455 Paradise Rd., Las Vegas, NV 89109

Tel 702–693–5090   Fax 702–693–5091

NOBU LONDON

Established February 1997—HOTEL METRO-POLITAN

19 Old Park Lane, London W1Y 4LB

Tel 020–7447–4747   Fax 020–7447–4749

NOBU TOKYO

Established October 1998—Aoyama

6-10-17 Minami Aoyama, Minato-ku, Tokyo

Tel 03–5467–0022   Fax 03–5467–0023

NOBU MALIBU

Established October 1999—Malibu Beach

3835 Crosscreek Rd., Malibu, CA 90265

Tel 310–317–9140   Fax 310–317–9136

NOBU MILANO

Established October 2000—Armani

Via Manzoni 31, 20121 Milano

Tel 02–72318645   Fax 02–72318674

UBON BY NOBU

Established November 2000—Canary Wharf

34 Westferry Circus, Canary Wharf, London E14 8RR

Tel 020–7719–7800   Fax 020–7719–7801

NOBU MIAMI

Established July 2001—South Beach

1901 Collins Ave., Miami Beach, FL 33139

Tel 305–695–3232   Fax 305–695–3219

"The famous Japanese actor Ken Takakura was my hero from school age onward. He is best known to Western audiences for his role as a Japanese cop opposite Michael Douglas in Ridley Scott's *Black Rain* (1989). In the limited free time I had working at Matsuei Sushi in Tokyo as an apprentice, I used to go and see his movies. I always empathized with his suave characters.

Soon after I opened Matsuhisa in Los Angeles, this distant hero of mine came to eat at the sushi counter. I was so nervous that all I could say at the end was that I hoped he had enjoyed his meal.

After I opened Nobu Tokyo, a radio broadcaster delivered a cassette tape and letter to me from Ken Takakura. It was a recording of an interview he'd given in which he read out part of a magazine article about me. I wanted somehow to say thank-you to him, so I contacted Mr. Shimamiya, an owner-chef of sushi restaurants in Sapporo who had been featured in the same radio program, and, through him, arranged a meeting with Ken. Since then Ken and I have kept in touch by phone, and he visits Nobu Tokyo whenever I'm in town. I still think his movies are great. There's something about his gritty determination that I find inspiring."

Dear Nobu-san,

It's been a long time, I must say, since my first visit to Matsuhisa in Los Angeles. Your restaurants are a success not only because of the delicious and exotic food you serve, but because of your personal experiences and the interesting people who have enriched your life. At your restaurants, customers can feel relaxed, inspired, and glad to be alive. You are truly a world-class chef, above and beyond the ordinary; you have given the world "Nobu," an out-of-this-world experience. I can't wait to see how you push even further our notions of "chef" and "cuisine" in the future.

Take care,

Ken Takakura

SUPPLIERS

NORTH AMERICA

WEST

Asahi-Ya
6541 Pacific Ave., Stockton, CA 95207
tel 209–464–9341

Ebisu Market
18940 Brookhurst St., Fountain Valley,
CA 92708
tel 714–962–2108

Eiko Market
14805 Jeffrey Rd. #E, Irvine, CA 92618
tel 949–551–3200

Imahara Produce & Japanese Foods
19725 Stevens Creek Blvd., Cupertino,
CA 95014
tel 408–257–5636

JapanGrocery.com
4126 Coleman Ave., San Diego, CA 92154
tel 877–219–8287
www.japangrocery.com

Maruwa Foods America Co., Ltd.
1746 Post St., San Francisco, CA 94115
tel 415–563–1901
www.maruwa.com

Mitsuwa Marketplace
333 S. Alameda St., Los Angeles,
CA 90013
tel 213–687–6699

Mitsuwa Marketplace
3760 Centinela Ave., Los Angeles,
CA 90066
tel 310–398–2113

Mitsuwa Marketplace
4240 Kearney Mesa Rd. #119, San Diego,
CA 92111
tel 858–569–6699

Mitsuwa Marketplace
665 Paularino Ave., Costa Mesa, CA 92626
tel 714–557–6699

Mitsuwa Marketplace
675 Saratoga Ave., San Jose, CA 95129
tel 408–255–6699

Mitsuwa Marketplace
21515 Western Ave., Torrance, CA 90501
tel 310–782–0335

Motoyama Market
16135 S. Western Ave., Gardena,
CA 90247
tel 310–324–0949

Nijiya Market
143 E. El Camino Real, Mountain View,
CA 94040
tel 650–691–1600

Nijiya Market
17869 Colima Rd., La Puente, CA 91748
tel 626–913–9991
fax 626–913–4990

Nippon Foods
2935 W. Ball Rd., Anaheim, CA 92804
tel 714–826–5321

Sakai K. Uoki Co.
1656 Post St., San Francisco, CA 94115
tel 415–921–0514
fax 415–921–0515

Spark Japanese Super Market
175 W. 25th Ave., San Mateo, CA 94403
tel 650–571–8620
fax 650–571–8629

Suruki Supermarket, Inc.
71 E. 4th Ave., San Mateo, CA 94401
tel 650–347–5288
fax 650–347–7548

Takahashi Market
221 S. Claremont St., San Mateo,
CA 94401
tel 650–343–0394

Tokyo Fish Market
1220 San Pablo Ave., Berkeley, CA 94706
tel 510–524–7243

Tokyo Market
3344 Kietzke Lane, Reno, NV 89502
tel 775–825–1533

PACIFIC NORTHWEST

Tokyo Foods
223 W. 7th Ave., Vancouver, BC V5Y 1L9
tel 604–879–0701

Uwajima Inc.
519 S. 6th Ave., Seattle, WA 98104
tel 206–624–6248

MIDWEST

Japan Imported Foods
808 NW. 6th St., Oklahoma City,
OK 73106
tel 405–235–8207

Mitsuwa Marketplace
100 E. Algonquin Rd., Arlington Heights,
IL 60005
tel 847–956–6699

EAST

Daikichi Mini-Market
122 E. 42nd St., New York, NY 10017
tel 212–661–3299

Fuji Mart Corp.
1212 E. Putnam Ave., Old Greenwich,
CT 06878
tel 203–698–2107

Fuji Mart Corp.
816 White Plains Rd., Scarsdale, NY 10583
tel 914–472–1468

Hamakko
88 Lincoln Hwy., Rahway, NJ 07065
tel 732–382–5628

Harajuku Inc.
238 E. Putnam Ave., Cos Cob, CT 06807
tel 203–552–0819

Jas Mart
2847 Broadway, New York, NY 10025
tel 212–866–4780

Katagiri & Co., Inc.
224 E. 59th St., New York, NY 10022
tel 212–755–3566
fax 212–752–4197

Kondo Grocery
314 E. 78th St., New York, NY 10021
tel 212–794–7065

Meiji-ya Trading Co., Inc.
18 N. Central Park Ave., Hartsdale,
NY 10530
tel 914–949–2178

Midori Mart Ltd.
2104 Chestnut St., Philadelphia, PA 19103
tel 215–569–3381
fax 215–569–3308
www.midorimart.com

Mitsuwa Marketplace
595 River Rd., Edgewater, NJ 07020
tel 201–941–9113

Nara Japanese Foods
169 Main St. #A, Port Washington,
NY 11050
tel 516–883–1836

Nara Japanese Gourmet Foods
109 Halstead Ave., Harrison, NY 10528
tel 914–835–0364

Nippan Daido USA, Inc.
1385 16th St., Fort Lee, NJ 07024
tel 201–944–0020

Nippan Daido USA, Inc.
522 Mamaroneck Ave., White Plains,
NY 10605
tel 914–683–6735

Oishinbo
283 Halstead Ave., Harrison, NY 10528
tel 914–835–4390

Shin Nippondo Corp.
63 Mineola Ave., Raslyn Heights, NY 11577
tel 516–625–1814

Sunrise Mart
4 Stuyvesant St., 2nd Fl., New York,
NY 10003
tel 212–598–3040

Toyo Foods
625 Port Washington Blvd., Port Washington, NY 11050
tel 516–944–6464

Yagura
24 E. 41st St., New York, NY 10017
tel 212–679–3777

Yoshinoya
36 Prospect St., Cambridge, MA 02139
tel 617–491–8221

SOUTH

Nippan Daido USA, Inc.
2390 Chamblee Tucker Rd., Chamblee,
GA 30341
tel 770–455–3846

Nippan Daido USA, Inc.
11146 Westheimer Rd., Houston,
TX 77042
tel 713–785–0815

UNITED KINGDOM

GREATER LONDON

Amaranth
346 Garratt Lane,
London SW18 4ES
tel 020–8871–3466

Arigato Japanese Supermarket
50 Brewer St.,
London W1R 3HN
tel 020–7287–1722

ASTA I
22-26 Broad Street Place, Eldon St.,
London EC2M 7JY
tel 020–7638–2404
fax 020–7628–5038

ASTA 2
6 Cutlers Gardens Arcade,
10 Devonshire Square,
London EC2M 4YP
tel 020–7626–8297
fax 020–7283–6671

ASTA 3
Beaufort House, 3 Middlesex St.,
London EC3A 7DT
tel 020–7247–7065
fax 020–7377–8924

Atari-Ya
595 High Rd., North Finchley,
London N12 ODY
tel 020–8446–6669
fax 020–8446–6728

Atari-Ya
7 Station Parade, Noel Rd.,
London W3 ODS
tel 020–8896–1552

Clearspring Ltd.
19A Acton Park Estate,
London W3 7QE
tel 020–8746–0152
fax 020–8811–8893
email mailorder@clearspring.co.uk
www.clearspring.co.uk
mail order

East-West Foods
Shop 3, The Oaks Shopping Centre,
High St., Acton,
London W3 6RE
tel 020–8992–7277

The Fifth Floor
Harvey Nichols, Knightsbridge,
London SW1X 7RJ
tel 020–7235–5000

Harro Foods Ltd.
Unit 23a, Lombard Rd.,
Merton, London SW19 3TZ
tel 020–8543–3343
fax 020–8542–1962
wholesale only

Harrods Food Halls
Knightsbridge, London SW1X 7XL
tel 020–7730–1234

Hoo Hing
Lockfield Ave., off Mollison Ave.,
Brimsdown, Enfield EN2 7QE
tel 020–8344–9888

Hoo Hing
Eastway Commercial Centre,
Eastway, Hackney, London E9 5NR
tel 020–8533–2811

Hoo Hing
Bond Rd., off Western Rd.,
Mitcham, Surrey CR4 3EB
tel 020–8687–2633

Hoo Hing
A406 North Circular Rd., nr Hanger Lane,
Park Royal, London NW10 7TN
tel 020–8838–3388

Hoo Hing
Commercial Centre, Chadwell Heath,
Romford, Essex RM8 1RX
tel 020–8548–3677

Loon Fung
1 Glacier Way,
Alperton, Middlesex HA0 1HQ
tel 020–8810–8188

Minamoto Kichoan
44 Piccadilly, London W1V 9AZ
tel 020–7437–3135
fax 020–7437–3191

Miura Foods
44 Coombe Rd., Kingston upon Thames,
Surrey KT2 7AF
tel 020–8549–8076
fax 020–8547–1216

Miura Foods
5 Limpsfield Rd.,
Sanderstead, South Croydon CR2 9AA
tel 020–8651–4498

Muji (Kensington)
157 Kensington High St.,
London W8 6SU
tel 020–7376–2484

Muji (Oxford Street)
187 Oxford St.,
London W1R 1AJ
tel 020–7437–7503

Muji (Soho)
41 Carnaby St.,
London W1V 1PD
tel 020–7287–7323

Natural House
Japan Centre, 212 Piccadilly,
London W1V 9LD
tel 020–7434–4218

Oriental City
399 Edgware Rd.,
Colindale, London NW9 0JJ
tel 020–8200–0009

Rice Wine Shop
82 Brewer St.,
London W1F 9UA
tel 020–7439–3705
fax 020–7439–3705

T. K. Trading
Unit 7, The Chase Centre,
8 Chase Rd.,
London NW10 6QD
tel 020–8453–1743
fax 020–8453–0606

Wing Yip
395 Edgware Rd.,
London NW2 6LN
tel 020–8450–0422
fax 020–8452–1478
email enquiry@wingyip.demon.co.uk

Wing Yip
554 Purley Way, Croydon CR0 4RF
tel 020–8688–4880

Yamazaki Bakery
Unit 2, Oriental City,
399 Edgware Rd., Colindale,
London NW9 OJJ
tel 020–8205–5569
fax 020–8205–9100

Yoshino
Unit 10, Oriental City,
399 Edgware Rd., Colindale,
London NW9
tel 020–8205–6500

SOUTHEAST

Akaneya
81 Northumberland Ave.,
Reading, Berkshire RG2 7PW
tel 0118–931–0448
fax 0118–975–7936
mail order

Midori
19 Marlborough Place,
Brighton, East Sussex BN1 1UB
tel 01273–601–460
fax 01273–620–422
www.midori.fsbusiness.co.uk
mail order

SOUTH

International Foods,
83-95 Derby Rd., Southampton,
Hampshire SO14 ODQ
tel 02380–220914
fax 02380–637007
www.internationalfoods.co.uk
mail order

SOUTHWEST

Jasmine
c/o Stanton House Hotel,
The Avenue, Stanton Fitzwarren,
Swindon, Wiltshire SN6 7SD
tel 01793–861–777
fax 01793–961–857

MIDLANDS

Wing Yip
375 Nechells Park Rd.,
Nechells, Birmingham B7 5NT
tel 0121–327–6618

Mountfuji International,
Felton Butler,
Nesscliff, nr Shrewsbury,
Shropshire SY4 1AS
tel 01743–741–169
www.mountfuji.co.uk
mail order

NORTH

Wing Yip
Oldham Rd.,
Ancoats, Manchester M4 5HU
tel 0161–832–3215

Harvey Nichols
107-111 Briggate, Leeds LS1 6AZ
tel 0113–204–8888

NORTHEAST

Setsu Japan (Angel Life Ltd.)
196A Heaton Rd.,
Newcastle upon Tyne NE6 5HP
tel 0191–265–9970
fax 0191–276–2951
mail order

AUSTRALIA

NEW SOUTH WALES

Japanese Food
G2d Tower Square,
155 Miller St.,
North Sydney, NSW 2059
tel (02) 9955–1090

Sydney Fish Market
Pyrmont Bridge Rd. (Cnr Bank St.),
Fish Market, Sydney NSW 2000
tel (02) 9660–1611
fax (02) 9552–1661

Tokyo Mart
Shop 27, Northbridge Plaza,
Northbridge, NSW 2063
tel (02) 9958–6860
fax (02) 9967–3152

Tokyo Mart Warehouse
Unit 3, 171 Gilbbes St.,
Chatswood, NSW 2057
tel (02) 9417–7200

VICTORIA

Prahran Market
163-185 Commercial Rd.,
South Yarra, VIC 3141
tel (03) 9522–3302
Tues & Sat: dawn to 5pm
Thurs & Fri: dawn to 6pm

Tokyo Mart
418 Glenhuntly Rd.,
Elsternwick, VIC 3185
tel (03) 9523–6200
fax (03) 9528–4120

GLOSSARY

aemono

Dressed foods. Cooked vegetables are generally served with a thick dressing made typically from sesame, tofu or miso in this basic category of Japanese cooking.

aji amarillo

This dried chili is orange, wrinkled, and tapers to a point. Its fruity flavor makes it suitable for chili sauces and stews. *Aji amarillo* paste is available as a commercial product in stores selling ingredients for South American cooking.

aji panca

This dried chili is dark brown, wrinkled, and tapers to a point. Its berry flavor and fruit tones make it suitable for chili sauces and fish dishes. *Aji panca* paste is available as a commercial product in stores selling ingredients for South American cooking.

anko-nabe

A one-pot stew in which monkfish meat, skin and liver are all simmered in a *dashi* made from monkfish bones. Monkfish is called *anko* in Japanese.

anticucho

A Peruvian dish. Beef heart is marinated in a red sauce, skewered and grilled over charcoal while being basted with oil. The meat is served with a yellow sauce and eaten with a salsa. (Page 79)

aori squid

This large squid (*Sepioteuthis lessoniana*)—called either oval squid or big fin squid in English—is prized for its thick, chunky meat, which makes excellent sashimi. As its alternative English name suggests, the *aori* squid has a large fin that can be as long as 6 inches (15cm). Its mantle is about 15 inches (40cm) long. *Aori* squid are caught in the seas around Japan and throughout the western Pacific, especially off the north coast of Australia and around Hawaii.

arrowroot

The king of starches, arrowroot is made from the swollen roots of *Maranta arundinacea*. Similar to potato flour or cornstarch (cornflour) in terms of its thickening properties, the more expensive arrowroot starch nevertheless produces superior results.

asatsuki chives

Similar to Chinese chives and scallions, *asatsuki* chives (*Allium ledebourianum*) can be shallow-fried as a vegetable or used as seasoning with sashimi.

ayu

This river fish (*Plecoglossus altivelis*) is caught with rod and line from June through August. Large specimens can be as long as 12 inches (30cm), but most are not even half that size. *Ayu* is usually eaten grilled or broiled with salt.

baby octopus

Baby octopus (*Octopus ocellatus*) is prized for its succulent meat in Japan. Smaller than the common octopus—a baby octopus will grow to no larger than 12 inches (30cm)—it is available fresh from late fall to early spring. During the winter months, the female will often contain fairly large eggs, which when cooked make the octopus look as if it has been stuffed with rice. This is why it's called *iidako* or "rice octopus" in Japanese.

bamboo shoot skin

Known as *take-no-ko* in Japanese, the shoots of both the *Phyllostachys heterocycla* and *Phyllostachys bambusoides* are a popular delicacy in Japan, often prepared as an *aemono* with *kinome*. The skin, which is usually peeled away before the shoots are boiled, can be used as an attractive garnish with strong hints of late spring.

bayberries

The purplish red fruit of the bayberry tree (*Myrica rubra*) is in season from late June to early July. The berries can be eaten raw, pickled in salt or made into jam or a liqueur.

beet (beetroot)

Beets have a distinctive earthy flavor that's enhanced by leaving the peel and some of the stem on while it's cooking. Varieties include the familiar red beets, golden beets, which turn a golden orange when cooked and are slightly sweeter than red beets, white beets, and candy cane beets which have alternating white and red rings inside.

benibana

The safflower (*Carthamus tinctorius*) was once used to produce orange and red pigments for dyeing. As well as being an attractive garnish for sashimi-style dishes, the safflower is also used to make a popular vegetable oil that is richer in polyunsaturated fats than any other oil. Originally a west Asian plant, this relative of the sunflower and thistle families is now cultivated in the drier regions of North Africa, China, India and the United States.

black cod

Also known as sablefish, black cod (*Anoplopoma fimbria*) is a dark-colored marine fish which is caught in North American Pacific waters from the Bering Sea to Isla Cedros, Baja California. Black cod can reach a length of 3 feet (90cm) and average 20 pounds (9kg) in weight. Due to its rich oil content, it is exceptionally flavorful and an excellent fish for smoking. Despite its name, this fish is not in fact a member of the cod family.

black rice

Black rice is a glutinous and ancient variety of Japanese rice with a purple-black pigment in the rice bran. It has a concentrated flavor.

blue crab

This blue-green crab (*Portunus trituberculatus*) is caught in the Tokyo and Ise Bays and the Ariake Sea from January through April. Measuring 6 inches (15cm) across, blue crab is filled with delicious meat which has a rich, sweet, succulent and buttery flavor. Blue crab is sold in both hard-shell and soft-shell forms. Peeler crabs are those taken just before molting; soft shell crabs are those harvested right afterward.

bonito flakes

Fileted bonito is steamed, dried, smoked and cured with a mold (*Aspergillus glaucus*). When the fillets have become as hard as a piece of wood, they are shaved. This whole process takes many months. The flakes are used to make *dashi* and as a flavoring and garnish in numerous other dishes. In fact, dried bonito flakes are necessary in one way or another for making every Japanese meal. Called *katsuobushi* in Japanese.

botan shrimp

The *botan* shrimp (*Pandalus nipponensis*) grows to about 6 inches (14cm) and is in season from October to May. It can be eaten raw, sautéed, deep-fried or as tempura.

buckwheat

Called *soba* in Japanese, this herbaceous plant (*Fagopyrum esculentum*) is cultivated for its groats. The husk is removed and used as a filling for pillows. The groats are ground into the flour that is used to make *soba* noodles. Groats can also be cooked with rice or used for making beer or vodka.

burdock root

Perhaps only the Japanese eat the burdock root (*Arctium lappa*) as a vegetable. A good source of dietary fiber, this 3-foot-3-inch- (1m-) long, 1-inch- (3cm-) thick root is peeled and soaked in cold water to remove its astringency. It can be combined with carrot to make *kinpira gobo*. Called *gobo* in Japanese.

ceviche

In this Central and South American specialty, raw fish is marinated in lime and lemon juice with olive oil and spices and served as an appetizer. (Page 118)

Chilean sea bass

Chilean sea bass (*Dissostichus eleginoides*) are not really bass but Patagonian toothfish, a large, slow-growing species first harvested in the early 1980s by Chilean longliners working the continental shelf in depths of 5,000 to 6,000 feet. It's a big fish; headed-and-gutted Chilean sea bass have weighed in at 100 pounds (45kg), but the average market weight is closer to 20 pounds (9kg). The fish is marketed in frozen form; "fresh" sea bass is nearly always "refreshed" (frozen fish that has been thawed). Chilean sea bass has a rich, melt-in-the-mouth flavor. The moderately oily meat is tender and moist with large, thick flakes. Meat from raw Chilean sea bass is snow white. When cooked, the meat remains white, comparable in appearance to cod. The Patagonian toothfish is also known as Antarctic cod and icefish.

chili garlic sauce

This fiery sauce is made from a blend of fresh, roasted or dried chilies and garlic, sugar, salt, vinegar and other seasonings.

chili oil

This hot, reddish orange oil is used as a flavoring agent and condiment. It is made by steeping dried red chilies in vegetable oil. It can be added to dishes to impart a fiery flavor or combined with milder oils and used to stir-fry.

Chinese chili bean sauce

This popular Chinese cooking sauce and condiment is made from a fermented brown bean sauce infused with mashed chili peppers, vinegar and other seasonings. Called *tobanjan* in Japanese, it adds an intense, fiery flavor and vivid red color to dishes.

Chinese salted black bean paste

A commercial paste made from black soybeans that have been fermented and preserved by salting.

cilantro (coriander)

Cilantro leaves are used throughout the world as a fragrant herb. Hispanic cooks use it in salsas, Asians in stir-fries, and Indians in curries. The seeds, stems and roots of the plant are also used. (Page 57)

daikon

The giant white radish (*Raphanus sativus*) is an essential ingredient in the Japanese larder. Grated *daikon* is added to the tempura dipping sauce because it aids the digestion of oily foods.

dashi

Japanese stock is made from dried bonito flakes and *konbu*. With soy sauce, saké and *miso*, it is one of the most important elements in Japanese cooking.

dogtooth violet

The leaves and flowers of the dogtooth violet (*Erythronium japonicum*) are commonly used as a garnish in Japanese cooking. Flour made from the plant is much prized as a starch and is sometimes used as an expensive alternative to potato flour.

eggplant (aubergine)

This spongy, mild-tasting vegetable is meaty yet low in calories. Japanese eggplants have thinner skins and a sweeter, more delicate flavor than American eggplants, and not as many of the seeds that tend to make them bitter. They're also usually more slender than American eggplants, but can vary in size and shape.

elephant garlic

Larger than regular garlic, elephant garlic (*Allium ampeloprasum*) is actually more closely related to the leek. Its large bulbs and mild flavor, however, account for its name. Commercially cultivated in the United States, impressive specimens can weigh more than 1 pound (450g) each.

enoki mushrooms

This winter mushroom (*Flammulina velutipes*) grows naturally worldwide, yet is known almost exclusively by its Japanese name. The sticky yellow-white cap is seldom wider than half an inch (1cm), while the long, thin stalks are usually well over 5 inches (12cm). *Enoki* mushrooms are used in soups, stews, and grilled with chicken. Fresh *enoki* are exported from Japan in sealed plastic packets that keep them fresh for a time.

fairy squid

As their name suggests, fairy squid (*Watasenia scintillans*) are tiny creatures which rarely grow longer than 2½ inches (7cm). Although they make their home at the bottom of the sea at depths between 100 and 550 fathoms (200–1000m), they come up to the surface for spawning from April through June each year. This is the only opportunity for fishermen to net substantial catches. Each fairy squid has over 800 luminous spots on its mantle, and the glowing catches in the fishermen's nets are a popular tourist attraction in Toyama prefecture on the Sea of Japan coast. For this reason, they are also sometimes known as firefly squid in English.

fiddlehead ferns

The young shoots of the ostrich fern (*Matteuccia struthiopteris*) are available canned, frozen and fresh. Their flavor has been described as a combination of broccoli, asparagus and globe artichoke.

filo

Filo is the Greek name for a paper-thin pastry that is used in many desserts from baklava to strudel. It is available already shredded and frozen from commercial suppliers.

flying fish roe

Also known as *tobiko* caviar, the tiny, bright orange, salted eggs of the flying fish have a mild, sweet, fishy flavor. Flying fish roe is used in small amounts as a tasty and decorative garnish for sushi and salads.

fruit tomatoes

Also known as sugar or perfect tomatoes, these small, sweet tomatoes can only be produced under special cultivation conditions which restrict the amount of water they are given. The yield is minimal, but their sugar content is as high as any fruit. Fruit tomatoes are not currently exported to the United States and Europe, and have been available in Japan for about ten years.

fugu

Fugu or blowfish is best known for its poison, and restaurant preparation of this fish is strictly controlled. Although it has been illegal to serve the *fugu*'s liver (the tastiest but most poisonous part) since 1984, there are regular deaths every year resulting from domestic preparation of *fugu* caught on a fishing trip or bought at the fish market.

futomaki

A thick roll of rice filled with egg, dried gourd shavings, cooked sea eel, mashed cooked fish and cucumber, wrapped in *nori* and cut into slices.

gari

Thinly sliced ginger marinated in sweetened rice vinegar is served as a condiment in sushi restaurants so diners can refresh their taste buds between different types of sushi.

green tea powder

Matcha—the tea used in the Japanese tea ceremony —is always sold as a powder that has to be mixed with hot water to make tea. It is available from Japanese markets and specialist tea merchants.

hajikami

These pickled ginger shoots are used to garnish many Japanese meals.

hamabofu

Hamabofu (*Glehnia littoralis*) grows in sand near the seashore. Its young leaves are eaten in the spring in boiled vegetable dishes. (Page 33)

hamachi

Young yellowtail (*Seriola quinqueradiata*) are called *hamachi* and adult yellowtail are called *buri* in Japanese.

hikarimono

The sushi chef's term for shiny sushi toppings such as mackerel.

hoba magnolia leaves

The leaves of the *hoba* magnolia or Japanese umbrella tree (*Magnolia hypoleuca*) are used to make a special *miso* paste and sometimes to wrap sushi.

ika somen

This popular summer dish consists of thin strips of squid, cut to resemble *somen* noodles, which are served raw with a dipping sauce and condiments like chopped scallions and grated ginger.

junsai

Sometimes called "water shield" in English, this tiny aquatic plant (*Brasenia schreberi*) has long, thread-like stems that grow up from the root. In early summer, the Japanese harvest the water shield's leafy shoots on the surface of ponds and pools. *Junsai* is sold loose in plastic bags or in bottles. (Page 28)

kabayaki

A broiled (grilled) dish in which the fish—usually a freshwater or sea eel—is opened up, boned, skewered and broiled while being basted with a thick, sweet sauce. The broiled fish is then usually served on a bowl of hot rice.

kaiware daikon

The young shoots of the *daikon* are used in salads and as a garnish for sushi. Cut off the root ends before using these sharp, spicy shoots.

king crab

This very large crab (*Paralithodes camtschaticus*)—more than 3 feet (1m) when spread out—is caught in the cod-fishing waters off the coast of Hokkaido from November through March. It is the largest of the commercially harvested crabs and is characterized by a spiny shell and long, spidery legs. King crabs can live for up to twenty years. Their meat is sweet, moist and rich.

kinome

Sansho sprigs are called *kinome* in Japanese. These young leaves are used as an edible garnish, chopped herb, or made into a paste. (See *sansho*)

konbu

Konbu (*Laminaria japonica*) is a variety of kelp that grows in the cold seas off the coast of northern Japan, mostly around the northern part of Hokkaido. Rich in monosodium glutamate, *konbu* is sold in supermarkets as *dashi konbu* in fairly large pieces for use in making stock. This *konbu* should never be washed because the flavor lies on the surface. At most, wipe it clean with a cloth and don't leave it in boiling water. *Konbu* is also a well-known dietary source of iodine and rich in iron.

kumazasa

The leaves of this diminutive species of bamboo (*Sasa albomarginata*) are commonly used as a garnish in Japanese cooking—especially in winter when the leaves are edged in white.

kuruma shrimp

Also called the tiger prawn (*Penaeus japonicus*), Japan's most popular shrimp can grow to a length of 8 inches (20cm). It is used as a sushi topping and also deep-fried in an egg-and-breadcrumb coating.

madako octopus

The common octopus (*Octopus vulgarus*) reaches an average size of 24–36 inches (60–90cm) in length. Called *madako* in Japanese, it can be found throughout the world's warm seas.

maitake mushrooms

This autumn mushroom (*Grifola fondosa*) is fragrant, tasty and very versatile. It is best in an *aemono* called *maitake no kurumi* in which the mushrooms are dressed with a walnut paste.

Maui onion

A hybrid onion named for the Hawaiian island in whose volcanic soil and cool climate this onion is at its sweetest.

menegi

The *wakegi* scallion (*Allium wakegi*) is specially cultivated to produce these young shoots which are used as a sashimi and sushi garnish. *Menegi* are harvested very soon after planting—perhaps only after three or four days—when the scallion has grown to a height of only 3 inches (8cm). They look much like—and can be substituted by—chives.

micro greens

This term refers to lettuces and other salad vegetables that are harvested at a very young age. The plants are picked as soon as small leaves have begun to appear, then washed and packaged in 4-ounce (100g) bags. Micro greens are available either individually or as a mixed assortment.

milt

This refers to the male reproductive glands of a fish when filled with secretion during the breeding season. A male fish ready for breeding is sometimes called a "milter."

mirin

This liquid flavoring containing 14% alcohol is used in cooking for its sweetness rather than its alcoholic content. Regular saké cannot be substituted for it.

miso

This fermented paste of soybeans and either rice or barley with salt is an essential ingredient in the Japanese larder. It is combined with *dashi* in *miso* soup and also used as a flavoring for other foods. Red *miso*, Japan's most popular rice *miso*, is salty and rich in protein; white *miso*, on the other hand, is rather sweet. Made from fermented soybeans and barley, *moromi miso* is never used for making *miso* soup. This soft, dark brown paste is usually eaten with chilled cucumber.

mizuame

Literally "water candy," *mizuame* is made by turning starch into sugar. It has the same consistency as maple syrup, but is completely colorless. *Mizuame* is also used as a sweetener in cooking when luster is required. Available at Asian supermarkets.

mizuna

This feathery, delicate salad green (*Brassica campeatris*) is a mildly peppery potherb that has been cultivated in Japan since antiquity.

mongo cuttlefish

The common cuttlefish (*Sepia officinalis*) and the pharaoh cuttlefish (*Sepia pharaonis*) are both called *mongo ika* in Japanese. The former grows to a maximum length of about 10 inches (25cm) and is familiar in the Mediterranean and east Atlantic. The latter is slightly larger and is prevalent from the Arabian Peninsula across to Japan and Australia.

moromi miso

A type of *miso* made from fermented barley, but never used for making *miso* soup. This soft, dark brown paste is most often eaten with chilled cucumber.

myoga ginger

Because only the stems and buds of *myoga* ginger (*Zingiber mioga*) are eaten, it is hardly recognizable as a type of ginger. It isn't hot like regular ginger and its fragrance is more herbal. The buds are especially aromatic when thinly sliced and used as a garnish.

nori

Red laver—*asakusa nori*—is harvested and dried in paper-thin sheets of a standard size. The *nori* is then toasted and used for wrapping sushi rolls, rice balls and *futomaki*. Green laver—*aonori*—is harvested, dried and sold in tiny flakes to sprinkle over food. *Aonori* is also an ingredient of *shichimi togarashi*.

North Pacific giant octopus

Found in the Pacific Ocean from California to Alaska to Japan, mature giant octopuses (*Octopus dofleini*) are generally caught in the 20–30 pound (10–15kg) range. Impressive specimens have been known to weigh about 600 pounds (270kg) and measure about 30 feet (9.6m) arm to arm. These large cephalopods are thought to live for three to five years at temperatures around 50°F (10°C). This is perhaps why they are called *mizudako* or "cold-water octopus" in Japanese.

o-hitashi

This dish of boiled vegetables is usually served chilled. Green vegetables are parboiled and then soused in *dashi* and seasoned with *mirin* and soy sauce.

okiuto

Okiuto is a processed food made from the *egonori* laver (*Campylaephora hypnaeoides*) found in Hakata Bay on the island of Kyushu. The laver is harvested in early summer, rinsed in cold water and dried in the sun. The process is repeated three or four times until the *nori* has hardened into thin blocks. A popular souvenir from Kyushu, *okiuto* is most often eaten as a breakfast dish with bonito flakes and soy sauce.

onion sprouts

More widely available in the United States than in Japan, onion sprouts are harvested after the onion has grown only about an inch during a twelve- or thirteen-day period. Similar to *kaiware daikon*, these sprouts have a distinct onion flavor.

pâte brique

This thin pastry originally comes from North Africa. The dough—consisting of water, flour, salt and vegetable oil—is boiled, making the surface rough, like a brick. Also called feuilles de briques, they are sold in circular sheets.

pleurote du panicaut

Pleurotus eryngii is a wild mushroom with a dark brown cap to be found between June and October, growing to a height of between 3 and 8 inches (7–20cm). Its flesh is firm and fragrant. Originally imported exclusively from Europe, this mushroom is now cultivated in Japan and sold as *eringi*.

ponzu

A citrus-and-soy-sauce dip.

red miso

Red *miso* (*akamiso*) is made from a fermented paste of soybeans and rice. It is red to brown in color and high in protein and salt.

red smartweed

Red smartweed (*Polygonum hydropiper*) is an extensively cultivated plant with a little purple leaf and a strong peppery flavor. Called *benitade* in Japanese, it is often mixed with soy sauce as a dip for sashimi or used as a garnish with other raw fish recipes.

red vinegar

This sweet and powerful rice vinegar made with saké lees that have been fermented with yeast and the *koji* mold (page 183) for three years is the preferred choice of sushi chefs, because relatively little sugar is needed to make the *shari-zu* for vinegared sushi rice.

rice vinegar

All vinegar produced in Japan is fermented from rice and is mild in flavor, with about 4.2% acidity. Non-rice vinegars cannot be used as substitutes.

rocoto chili paste

Also known as rocotillo, this relation of the habanero is orange-yellow or deep red when ripe, round with furrows, and tapering to a point. It is mildly fruity and has an intense heat. Essential for ceviches, rocoto chili paste is available as a commercial product in stores selling ingredients for South American cooking.

saka-mushi

A Japanese cooking technique that involves steaming seafood with saké.

salmon roe (salmon eggs)

These shiny red eggs are considered a luxury and taste excellent when served as sushi or simply as a topping on hot rice.

sansho

The seedpods of the Japanese pepper (*Zanthoxylum piperitum*) are ground and used as seasoning, especially as one of the seven spices in *shichimi togarashi*. The *sansho* is usually sold ground, as it keeps its fragrance quite well. *Sansho* sprigs (the young leaves are called *kinome* in Japanese) can be used as an edible garnish, chopped herb, or made into a paste.

scallions (spring onions)

These immature green onions are harvested before they have formed bulbs or while the bulbs are still small. With a peppery onion flavor, scallions are used mainly as a condiment in Japanese cooking.

sea urchin

This creature's spiny shell (or more correctly "test") makes it look an unappetizing treat for predators. Cut the sea urchin open horizontally and you will find five orange or rose-colored ovaries. These ovaries or corals are considered a great delicacy in Japan and can be eaten on their own, used as a sushi topping or as an ingredient in sauces. The French have a special implement for cutting the sea urchin called a *coupe-oursin*. The ovaries are also available already separated from the test. Called *uni* in Japanese.

shabu-shabu

A Japanese one-pot dish of thinly sliced beef and vegetables. *Shabu-shabu* is almost always cooked and served at the table. Diners use chopsticks to swish the beef slices and vegetables in simmering *dashi* and then eat the morsels with a dipping sauce. *Shabu-shabu* is the sound made as the beef is swished about in the *dashi*. (Page 31)

shari

The rice part of sushi.

shari-zu

The vinegar mixture used to make vinegared sushi rice.

shichimi togarashi

This "seven-spice mixture" is a snappy collection of seven dried and ground flavors: red pepper flakes, roughly ground *sansho*, tiny flakes of mandarin orange peel, black hemp seeds, tiny flakes of green *nori* and white sesame seeds. Available in three strengths—mild, medium and hot—from Asian supermarkets.

shiitake mushrooms

The best-known Japanese mushroom (*Lentinus edodes*) is extensively cultivated and often available in its dried form. Its distinctive pungent flavor goes well with Japanese food. Fresh *shiitake* are good as tempura, in stews or simply grilled with a little salt.

shimeji mushrooms

This autumn mushroom (*Lycophyllum shimeji*) is known for its excellent flavor rather than its aroma. It has straw-colored caps about ¼ inch (1cm) in diameter.

shio-kara

A salt-cured preserve of fish, molluscs and their entrails. Squid is the most popular *shio-kara*, but sea urchin *shio-kara* is produced and consumed in large quantities in western Japan.

shiso

There are both red and green *shiso* leaves. The red ones (*akajiso*) are mainly used to color *umeboshi* and other pickles. The green leaves (*aojiso*) have many uses as a herb, tempura and garnish. Although it is called a perilla or beefsteak plant (*Perilla frutescens*) in English, *shiso* is actually a member of the mint family. *Shiso* buds are also used as a condiment, garnish and, when very young, for tempura.

snow crab

This large crab (*Chionoecetes opilio*) is caught in the Sea of Japan in the winter months and served as sashimi, tempura and in vinegared preparations. Snow crab meat is sweet and delicate, with a more fibrous texture than king crab. Its texture ranges from the tender longitudinal fibers of shoulder meat to the firmer fibers of claw meat.

soba

Buckwheat noodles can be eaten either hot or cold. In their simplest form, a *dashi*-based soup is poured over the boiled noodles for *kake-soba*. When eaten cold, the noodles are served on a bamboo sieve with a dipping sauce. This is called *zaru-soba* (*zaru* being the Japanese for bamboo sieve). (Page 88)

somen

These dried, fine wheat noodles are served cold with a chilled dipping sauce usually in the summer. The noodles are boiled very briefly and then immediately refreshed in cold water. (Page 25)

spiny lobster

Japanese spiny lobsters (*Panulirus japonicus*) are almost always less than 12 inches (30cm) in length nowadays because of overfishing in Japanese waters. They lack the large front claws of the American lobster and are prized instead for their tail meat, which accounts for 33% of the body weight. The tail meat is firm, mild and

sweet. As well as making excellent sashimi, it is delicious when split in half and simply grilled. Called *ise-ebi* in Japanese.

su-miso

White *miso* paste thinned with rice vinegar is often used as a dressing in *aemono*.

sudachi

This acidic citrus fruit (*Citrus sudachi*) is a smaller relative of *yuzu*. It is used in the summer and autumn while still green for its tangy juice and aromatic zest. *Sudachi* is rarely available outside Japan and lemons can be used as a substitute.

tabbouleh

This Middle Eastern salad is typically made of parsley, tomato and burgul with scallions, mint, oil, lemon juice and seasoning.

tardivo radicchio di Treviso

One of two quality varieties of radicchio (a type of chicory) from the Treviso region of northern Italy. The tardivo has pronounced ribs and splayed leaves. It is very pretty and more flavorful than the other varieties.

tataki

A way of serving bonito or beef in which fillets are seared, leaving the inside raw, and sliced like sashimi. The fillets are then topped with finely chopped white scallions and served with Tosa-zu (page 173).

tiradito

Tiradito is a South American dish consisting of cut fish and ceviche seasonings. Its name is derived from *tirar* (the Spanish for "throw") because the fish slices are thrown into the serving bowl. (Page 120)

tomyo pea sprouts

Chinese pea shoots (*dau miui* and *dou miao*) are the handpicked, tender leaves and stems of the snow or garden pea plants, and are used as a light seasoning or added to soups. In Japan, *tomyo* pea sprouts are cultivated hydroponically and produced throughout the year in bulk. Pea sprouts are more aromatic and delicately flavored than bean sprouts.

toro

The belly of tuna is very pale in color and fatty. Highly prized for sushi and sashimi, it is considered the best cut of the fish.

udo

The white stalks and leaves of this aromatic plant (*Aralia cordata*) are similar to asparagus in taste and smell. The tender young stems can be eaten raw or boiled in *aemono* or *o-hitashi*.

udon

These soft, thick wheat noodles are eaten in bowls of a *dashi*-based soup with tempura and other accompaniments.

ume

This early summer fruit (*Prunus mume*) is often mistakenly called a plum when in fact it is an apricot. It is salt-pickled to make *umeboshi* or macerated with rock sugar in alcohol to make a liqueur called *umeshu*.

umeboshi

Dried salt-pickled Japanese apricots are a staple of the Japanese diet. Start the morning with a cup of *bancha* tea containing an *umeboshi* or place one on top of the

rice in your *bento* (lunch) to create a *hinomaru bento*. ("Hinomaru" is the name of the Japanese national flag.) (Page 76)

wakame

This seaweed (*Undaria pinnitifida*) is used in *miso* soup, salads and other dishes.

wasabi

Although similar in flavor, Japanese horseradish (*Wasabia japonica*) is less harsh and more fragrant than its English cousin. Fresh *wasabi* is very expensive. It grows wild in cool, shallow pools of pure water, often high in the mountains, and is extensively cultivated under similar conditions. It can also be bought as a powder or paste from Asian supermarkets.

white miso

White *miso* (*shiromiso*) is made from a fermented paste of soybeans and rice or barley. It is beige to light brown in color and quite sweet. A high-grade Kyoto product, white *miso* is expensive.

yakitori

Bite-size pieces of chicken grilled on a skewer. All of the chicken is used, including the skin, liver and gizzard.

yamagobo root

The young, edible roots of a woodland thistle called *mori azami* (*Cirsium dipsacolepis*) bear a striking resemblance to burdock, even though there is no direct relation between these flora. *Yamagobo* roots are typically pickled in *miso* or soy sauce and used as a filling in *futomaki* and other sushi rolls.

yanagi matsutake mushrooms

This wild mushroom (*Agrocybe cylindracea*) is found at the foot of willow and maple trees between spring and fall. It has a dark brown cap and grows to a height of between 4 and 6 inches (10–15cm). Its flesh is firm and crisp. Sometimes marketed as a *shakkiri* mushroom, nowadays it is cultivated and sold throughout the year. It is not related to the more famous and expensive *matsutake* mushroom.

yariika squid

Yariika or spear squid (*Loligo bleekeri*) is a slender, spear-shaped cephalopod which grows to about 15 inches (40cm) in length. Spear squid are caught in the seas around Japan, particularly in the spring when they come close to the coast to lay their eggs.

yuba

The skin that forms on the surface of soy milk when heated is the richest known source of protein (over 50%) and similarly high in natural sugars and polyunsaturated fats. Eaten both fresh and dried, most *yuba* is made in Kyoto and can be quite expensive. (Page 113)

yuzu

Japanese citron (*Citrus junos*) is zestier than lemons and not as sweet. *Yuzu* also has a very potent fragrance. It is used for both its acidic juice and its aromatic rind. Yuzu juice is now available in bottles from Asian supermarkets.

yuzu kosho

Available from Japanese markets, this commercial seasoning comprises green chili pepper, *yuzu* rind and salt.

INDEX